I Just Wanna Be Somebody

A Collection of Literary Monologues

Pamela Pfister

First Edition
Available in Softcover and on Kindle

So Blest Publishing
Pensacola, Fl 32533

Cover design by Mac McGovern, Pensacola, Fl
Photography by Hartman Photography, Pace Fl

All rights reserved. ISBN-13:978-0692492352
(So Blest Publishing)
ISBN-10: 0692492356

I lovingly dedicate this book to my grandchildren:

Megan Saum Fountain, Collin Saum; Emily, Samuel, Jeremy, Kira, Kendi, Gift, and Melody Saum; Matthew, Kennedy, and Elizabeth Pfister; and Andrew Platt

Table of Contents

Special Acknowledgements

A very special thanks to Mac McGovern, President of the West Florida Literary Federation, Pensacola Florida. He helped format, edit, and idealize this book. His knowledge and expertise has been priceless to me.

I would also like to thank my writing class at the Cultural Center in Pensacola for their input and critiquing me through the writing of the stories in this book. Thank you Andrea, Heidi, Tabbi, Ann, Richard, Dr Fabian, and Edward.

I Just Wanna Be Somebody

A Collection of Literary Monologues

Anne, the Aviator

VFR and IFR Pilots

What if you had been frozen for the past 50 years, and just thawed? You would have to learn the prevailing code of operation in this life. You would have to learn the existing vocabulary. For example, "HDTV," "DVR," "VIP" or H-2-o. How about "MPV" or "LCD" or PIP"? Am I communicating? Our stock of words has taken on a new implication.

Pilot lingo resembles this new code talk. There is a VFR pilot and an IFR pilot. The IFR rating is the most desirable. I will explain.

The instrument flight rated pilot (IFR) has more flying hours and intense training. The instrument panel has to be mastered. The IFR pilot must trust the panel explicitly. It is similar to flying blindfolded. In fact, in training he may be blindfolded at times because situations at hand may prohibit the pilot from seeing anything outside the plane. When he is in a cloud, or in hazardous weather, or at nighttime, vision is greatly impaired, (to say the least!)

A visual flight rated pilot (VFR) does not know everything about the instruments, so he "flies by sight." He has to see what's going on in the skies around him. If the VFR man gets in a cloud, he is a blind man. He must stay under the clouds. That is called "scud running." There is a cloud over his head all the time. He can accidentally get "in the soup" if he flies into a cloud. However, the IFR pilot is flying above the clouds and soaring with the eagles.

Can I get eye to eye with you and talk about this? Pilots say, "Can I level with you?"

I know people who live below the clouds all the time and their life is just like a scud runner. The instrument panel which must be trusted so unquestionably is analogous to the Bible. As the instrument panel guides you to your destination, the Bible is a marvelous life guide to eternity. It is called, "Living by faith and not by sight."

Can I give you a lift? C'mon up a little higher where the sun is shining. There is an elevation which pilots term "CAVU: "Clear and vision unlimited."

That is what I call "Flyin' High!" You can do it with a little more instruction. I am Anne the Aviator, and I am here to be your life coach.

Attitude VS. Altitude

I'm on top of the world, looking down on creation and I'm passionate about flying! In fact, I get ecstatic when I'm airborne. Yes indeed, I was born to soar. Chocolates are presented to new mothers in the hospital, but "Air Heads" were bestowed to Mom when I was born!

Today I filed my flight plan with the control tower. Flying is not a que sera sera operation. Whatever will be, will be. Every detail of the flight must be reported to the tower after a flight is executed on paper.

For example, the point of departure must be given along with the point of destination. What is the estimated time of arrival? At what altitude will the plane be flying? What is the gross weight? How many souls are on board?

When the plane is up, up, and away, the air traffic controller will ask, "What is your attitude?"

He is not asking if you are in a good mood or bad mood. He wants to know the position of the plane. Are your wings level?

For example, I might ask you about your attitude as a pedestrian. You may talk about your feelings, your disposition, or state of mind. Henceforth, the attitude is the posture of a person, as is the position of the plane. Sit up straight! Chin up! Pull the tummy in! Be high-minded! You can fly above the bad weather by thought ascension. Get your thoughts out of the mud. Did you know your life could go in the direction of your most prominent thoughts?

The Bible says to "set your mind on things above, not on things of earth," (Colossians 3:2). You cannot be down in the dumps when you are navigating on life's journey.

To sum it up, live upward. Look higher.

To settle for being earthbound when you can soar with the eagles, would be mayhem to your destiny. Strike an attitude! I am Anne, the Aviator and I can help you to be an overcomer. I can help you make your attitude your altitude. How about a lift?

The Checklist

The bumper sticker on my car reads, "I'd rather be flying!" I love looking down on creation. When you are an aviator, people look up to you. (Get it?) Seriously, it takes education, practice, and discipline to be an accomplished pilot. It is called "higher learning!"

A pilot is never alone. There is someone in the control tower watching the plane at all times. The plane is on the radar screen, and the air traffic controller has the identification number, precisely, as in "4209-er Romeo." He is responsible for guiding the plane through weather, air traffic, and unforeseen problems. Every word and movement is under video surveillance.

One of the earliest acts I remember in ground school was the "walk-around." It is a flight list to check off the many parts and aeromechanics of the plane. This is a charge, a call of duty, a matter of course in preparing for takeoff. It is never considered redundant.

There is one more thing on the agenda before takeoff...the passengers. The concern of each flight is preparation and safety. What if some unforeseen event overtakes this flight and we all go down together? How is your heart? Are you prepared to meet your Maker?

All earthlings are under video surveillance by "Jehovah's Tower of Royal Power." There is such a thing as the final approach. Life consists of practice takeoffs and landings. Pilots call it "go-arounds."

This could be the final debut into eternity and it

is my duty to inform you and warn you that life is an emergency. Prepare!

I have often thought it would be a good idea if pedestrians started the day with a "check list" and "walk-around."

My mom had her personal check list. "Did you go to the bathroom?" "Did you wash your hands?" "Did you remember to say 'Thank you?'" "Did you take the trash out?" Nevertheless, if we would do diligence today, the assignment might unfold like this.

We are trinity beings, spirit, soul, and body. The body has a daily regimen. It's not hard to remember to brush your teeth and put on deodorant, dress appropriately and look the best you can.

There is a "Things To Do" list for the soul, and the mind also. The mind must be prepared to regulate its degree of readiness for the daily combat of life. Inspiration and motivation are helpful to begin the day.

Next is the eternal part of a person, the spirit. The Bible talks about "putting on the whole armor of God." It is defensive clothing. It is spiritual, not physical. It is given to resist and stand your ground on the evil day of danger. Stand, having tightened the belt of truth, the breastplate of integrity and right standing with God.

Your feet should be prepared to face the enemy with firm footed stability which is produced by the Gospel of peace. The shield of faith can quench the fiery darts from the enemy. The helmet of salvation is protection for the head, and the sword of the Spirit is the Word of God.

That completes the checklist for the pedestrian and the pilot. I am Anne, the aviator, and I am here to help make your life's journey an enjoyable adventure. I've got high hopes!

Marigold the Gardener

Oh, To Be Like A Dandelion

Cr-ack! Sp-lit! Ch-ip! Um-ph! By tenacity and toughness, the tender dandelion comes bursting through a ton of asphalt pavement. With true grit, the fragile weed flower makes its debut into the world of sunshine and fresh air, providing every little child their mother's first bouquet.

What kind of life force or "tough stuff" is this little resolute weed made of? The energy driving the dandelion comes from its "cambium," a layer in the seed that is 100% spunk. It produces enough "push" to break through and crack a cement sidewalk or a blacktop drive.

The cambium equips the dandelion with more vigor than a human dynamo. Of course, the dandelion is not alone in creation to be endowed with such hardihood. Nevertheless, its saw-toothed leaves and generic golden blossoms inspire me as they break through. It is a quality lacking in much of the human race. The valor of this common weed flower does not end with its dauntless debut or should one say, "It's coming out party?"

Everyone knows of its persistence. If the grass in the front yard is 2" high, the dandelion will grow to be 3" high. If the yard is neglected and the grass gets to be 10" high, the not-to-be whipped dandelion will grow 11" high.

A dandelion is happy to bloom anywhere. It blossoms early in the morning and closes at evening. It works early till late. Employers are looking for that "dandy" trait, but it is a rare virtue found in people.

It simply will not be downed. It rises above its

circumstances. Remember the dandelion the next time problems get you down. The dandelion is not easily discouraged. It does not wilt with sorrow if it has to bloom behind a barn. It does not grow any brighter yellow or taller on the courthouse lawn or at the city dump.

The flowers, when they ripen, form cottony seeds which the wind carries to produce hundreds and thousands more of its kind. It does not need to be pollenated by another flower or insect. Everything needed to reproduce itself is within the flower.

There is an interesting analogy here. Believers have "Christ within, the hope of glory." When King David was at his lowest point in life and no one was there to cheer him, the Bible says, "He encouraged himself." Inside of him was everything he needed to get up, and get going. His son, Solomon, wrote, "The righteous shall prosper like the palm tree." The older the palm tree becomes, the better the fruit is. The older the dandelion, the more flowers it reproduces!

It seeks every nook and corner to grow and smile and prepare its seed. If a dandelion has been endowed with such purposefulness, how much more of a mission must exist within each person? Constantly seek opportunities to bring the seed of hope to others. What a fertile spot every place presents!

Dandelions do not have pity parties. Whoever heard of a "blue dandelion?" I have never heard one crying a tune, "I'm not a white hyacinth, a red rose, or a purple violet!"

No, they always tell the same golden story.

It brings that yellow out of a black soil and makes the best of what it has been given.

What is so difficult about "blooming where we are planted?"

Flowers are symbols of certain feelings and emotions. For instance, violets symbolize faithfulness, lilies purity, daises innocence, and orange blossoms-good luck. The dandelion is the epitome of sticking it out. The next time you see this little plant, take heart. They may be a troublesome weed and difficult to control, but their existence is with objective. And so is yours.

Nature reveals the secrets of righteousness. "The heavens declare the glory of God; and the firmament show His handiwork." Psalm 19:1 .

"Lord, help us to have the resolution of the dandelion!"

The Bonsai and Sequoia Tree

The Japanese grow a traditional tree which dates back over a thousand years. Called the Bonsai (bon'si') tree, beautiful and perfectly formed, its height is measured in inches!

In California, there are forests of giant trees called Sequoias. One of these giant trees has been named "General Sherman." It is 272 feet high and 79 feet around. If it were cut down, it would produce enough lumber to build thirty-five, five room homes! At one time, the Bonsai tree and General Sherman were the same size! When they were seeds, each weighed less than 1/300th of an ounce.

When the Bonsai tree first came bursting out of the ground, the Japanese pulled it from the soil, tied its taproot, some of the feeder roots and deliberately stunted its growth. The result, a miniature, dwarfed tree. The seed of the sequoia, General Sherman, was nourished by the minerals of the soil, the rain, and the sun.

They did not have a choice in their destiny. But YOU do! The miraculous feature of human life is the ability to change, the power of choice, if you will. It is the miracle of transformation through salvation.

Removing ceilings and road stops to obtain the good things in life are a choice. You may have been conditioned in the past...taught, trained, molded. But if you really have the desire to grow and be what you were meant to be, you have the awesome power of choice, which ultimately brings change.

One good decision, one good selection after another will make a better tomorrow. Enough good tomorrows will bring a happy and successful future. Bonsai or Sequoia? It is your preference.

GENERAL SHERMAN

© Jonathan Fay 2012

A Goober's Perspective

Peanuts are like people. All of them have a crook in their life somewhere. Some are badly bent, others are fairly straight. None are absolutely perfect. The peanut is unusual because it flowers above the ground but fruits below the ground. There are misconceptions how peanuts grow, completely different from the root of the potato or trees such as walnuts and pecans.

Peanut seeds grow into a green oval-leafed plant about eighteen inches tall and develop delicate flowers around the lower portion of the plant. The flowers pollinate themselves, and then lose their petals. They grow downward away from the plant, and extend into the soil.

The peanut is equipped with a double covering. The outside is the one the public sees. It is harder and tougher than the inner one, which is a thin covering of the nut itself. The inner one is not seen until the outer one is broken.

People are like peanuts, with a true inner person and an outer shell seen by society.
There is a saying, "Your front yard is your reputation, but your backyard is your character."

Solomon, one of the wisest men who ever lived, wrote, "Who can make that straight which God has made crooked?" Man cannot make the peanut straight. It has a crooked design. Humans can be very contrary, too. But the peanut has no value until it is broken. Roses have to be crushed to make perfume. Animals have to die to give their meat for food, their skins for clothing.

When the shell is broken, the heart can be reached. In regard to human beings, the heart is the core and the essence of emotions. The heart changes the countenance for good or for evil.

Every peanut has a sweet heart. In fact, there are two hearts in each peanut. People always have a "heart" for something. Some have a change of heart. Some have a broken heart. Some wear their heart on their sleeve.

Some are hearty, and others heartless. Friedrich Nietzsche wisely stated, "One ought to hold on to one's heart; for if one lets it go, one soon loses control of the head too."

To have the heart in the wrong place is detrimental to success in life.

All peanuts are the same color on the outside. It is said that color speaks all languages. But on the inside, all are transparent, easily seen. People could be much more approachable if the inner person was not so obscure.

Is it not intriguing that the Creator of the peanut and the person has become pre-occupied with His creation and given His full-time attention to the comings and goings and provision of mankind? If He can make His entrance through the door of the heart of individuals, He naturally causes them to have compassion and concern for others. As the peanut pollinates itself, so do people fertilize or pollute their world. It is interesting to note that the peanut provides enrichment and nutrition to the plant and soil around it. Can we affect our environment so positively?

The peanut cannot be made straight. But people have an alternative to life's "crooked paths." There is a "straight and narrow" way, which is a change in elevation and an upgrade to existence. The next time someone denotes the goober and says, "Oh, that's just peanuts!" I hope you will speak up and say, "I beg to differ!"

Wella the Nurse

We All Need To Cry

Crying is not a mistake! We need to cry three different kinds of tears. Boohooing is essentially a 0.9% solution of water and salt. Crying flushes out concerns. Everyone feels better after a good cry. You can brush your teeth, swab your ears, shampoo your hair, bathe your body, but how do you get your eyes clean? Tears! They wash and lube your eyes.

When you blink, your eyes are washed with tears made in two little almond-shaped organs above each of your eyes called lachrymal (lac-rim-al) glands. Your eyelids are lined with a body oil to keep them from leaking out. Tears flow to a drain called the tear duct. They flow into your nose and then down to your mouth. That's why you taste saltiness when you cry.

There are essential reasons for those tears that flow, and there are three different kinds of teardrops. The first kind is basal tears, the all-time tears, 24/7. They include antibiotics and oils that protect and keep your eyes lubricated.

Reflex tears have more antibiotics plus enzymes than the 24/7 basal tears and can break down invading chemicals. When your eyes are bothered by irritants such dust or the smell from onions, reflex tears are called to the scene.

Psychogenic tears include all of the above plus higher amounts of the proteins that increase when you are under stress. Harmful chemicals that build up inside can be released during crying, and these are tears from emotion or stress overload.

The next time you feel sorry for yourself and the

tears begin to well up, it might be good to remind yourself of the importance of your tears to Someone. Yes, King David said God bottles his tears (Ps. 56:8) But then, He is going to wipe all tears away in the by and by. (Rev. 7:17)

The status of exceptionalism which endows you with perpetual moisture supplies can be attributed to the marvel of creation.

The instrument of sight is a fascination beyond extraordinary. At first observation, you may think your eyes are just an accessory, but they are indeed a celebration of genius creative design. For crying out loud, give a "wink" and a "thank you" to your Heavenly Ophthalmologist for vision equipage that is amazing!

Rx: Laughter

What you need is a good internal massage! A big belly laugh gently massages internal organs, something many people do not get. The muscles that get a workout during laughter are those in the chest, abdomen, shoulders, neck, face and scalp. You've heard it said, "I laughed so hard, I cried?"

The contraction of the muscles of the eye squeeze tears from the tear glands and interfere with their natural drainage through tear ducts and into the upper nose.

Therefore, tears overflow the eye and trickle down the cheeks during heavy laughing.

What about "I laughed so hard, I wet my pants!" Muscle contraction around the bladder can produce life's most embarrassing moments. Laughter is followed by a general reduction of muscle tension. You get rid of greater amounts of carbon dioxide as your lungs complete their air exchange duties. Taking in some oxygen- rich air causes the red blood to go to the cells with the oxygen. People turn red or crimson with laughter.

During laughter there is an increase in rapid brain wave behavior which causes greater alertness and cerebral functioning. Laughter also kills pain by stimulating the secretion of endorphins, the body's natural anesthetics.

Medical professionals are now looking more closely at the role of laughter in human longevity and the healing process. They're finding it is "no laughing matter."

Norman Cousins wrote a book in 1979, "Anatomy of An Illness." The book spent 40 weeks on the New York Times best-seller list.

It told how he recovered from a crippling disease by tapping into the power of laughter. He rented videos of The Three Stooges and doubled up in laughter, and the healing began inside. Having a good emotional support system and a positive attitude with humor as a key role will prolong life.

There is a little story that might tickle your innards. The first church downtown advertised for a steeple bell ringer. A little hunchback man with no arms applied for the job. "I can do it. Just watch me." He backed up and got a running start and cabonged the bell with his head. He was hired. For weeks everything went well.

The Church bells chimed beautiful echoing their tune throughout the community. Then came the Sunday dilemma.

The pastor delivered a most inspiring message. All the deacons and elders were seated in the two front rows, right and proper. Immediately following the benediction, the church bells were to chime. And they did...beautifully. But then the loudest clatter and rumble and thud came from the bell tower.

Here comes the armless hunchback bell ringer thumping and snorting and crashing down the stairway, skidding down between the altar and the front row of deacons and elders. One of the deacons turned to another and said, "What in the world? Who is this?" The other deacon replied, "I don't know. But his face rings a bell!"

"A merry heart does good like a medicine," says Proverbs 17:22. And it is a cosmetic plus says Proverbs 15:13, "A merry heart makes a cheerful countenance." Not to mention it is an energy booster says Nehemiah 8:10, "The joy of the Lord is our strength." It takes three minutes of hard rowing to double the heart rate. It takes laughter about twenty seconds.

Want to do a little internal jogging? Here is a story about a little old lady with feelings of timidity. She and her husband were preparing for a camping trip in a neighboring town in their state.

She wrote the Chamber of Commerce because she wanted to know if the campground had inside facilities. She thought asking if they had toilets would sound uncouth.

Bathroom commodes were still too unrefined.

She wrote, "Do you have a "B.C.?" When they received the letter they passed it around the office. It puzzled everyone. What could she be referring to? It must be Baptist Church. Fire her a letter back and tell her "Yes, we do have a "B.C." Visitors are welcome. Some folks bring their lunch and stay all day.

There are special activities for singles and seniors. Treats for the children. You'll never meet a stranger there. Doors are open from 8 A.M. to 8 P.M. Bring a friend!"

You do not have to work as hard to be happy, versus the alternative, being unhappy. It has been determined it takes more muscles to frown than to smile. So smile awhile and give your face a rest!

Dress for Stress SUCCESS!

Nothing is worth more than this day," writes Goethe. Look well to this one day, for it and it alone is life. It has been quoted, "Today is the first day of the rest of your life." If today is more important than any other, don't you think you should dress for it? Of course, the apparel for the inner and the outer man bears no similarity.

The inner person wears gear in preparation to face the day and it is called a "habit", which is a garment worn by the personality. In Isaiah 61:3 it says "Put on the garment of praise for the spirit of heaviness."

You can usually tell what the inner person is wearing by the "spokes" that come out of the mouth!

The emotion wardrobe closet includes stress, distress, and eustress. Resting on your shoulders is the one in charge of decisions. You decide what you'll put on from the emotion closet. "Know first who you are, and then adorn yourself accordingly," says Thomas W. Higginson.

Stress befits much of the population. It may be the mode of the day but it is not becoming nor healthy. Stress is a body's method of reacting to a challenge. The term "stress" is derived from a Middle English word "distresse." It means to "draw tight." The stress emotion releases a chemical, cortisol, which damages and kills neurons in the brain. It can be tied to deterioration or decline of memory often experienced with age. Chronic stress impairs healing and affects immunity. Worry and stress are the inner man's coat and cloak.

If we could see into the future, all of our problems in their true light wouldn't seem so critical. If the things people worry about could be relegated to their true size, stress would not be so pressing. According to the Bureau of Standards, a dense fog covering seven city blocks, 100 feet deep, if contained in a single drinking glass, would not quite fill it. You could probably put your worries into a water glass, too.

If stress is not the choice, then distress is another inner garment wrought by high strung emotion. Distress or anxiety suffered is a response to a sudden, severe, and saddening experience. Who wants to put on great pain, anxiety or sorrow, acute physical or mental suffering, affliction and trouble? No thanks!

There is yet another "habit" or internal garment to choose. It is "eustress," the good stress. It is described as moderate or normal psychological stress interpreted as being beneficial for the experiencer. Eustress is the feeling you get when overcome with excitement and anticipation of a desired outcome.

It is important for us to have it and without it we would become depressed and feel a lack of meaning in life. It enhances strength training, challenges, and helps an individual continue working and remaining healthy.

"The apparel often proclaims the man," says Shakespeare. Napoleon said "A man becomes the creature of his uniform." So, you see, the outside affects the inside, as well as the inside affecting what is visible to the eye. You become what you mostly think about. Stress has its origin in the mind. Its management must be accomplished by attention, care, and bringing thoughts under control. This is your jurisdiction.

"As a man thinks, so is he."

But a person who has good thoughts cannot even be ugly. You can have a wonky nose and crooked mouth, and double chin. But if you have good thoughts-then you will shine, and your face will look like sunbeams. And you will be lovely!

Beauregard, the Peddler

Real Estate to Die For

Have I got a deal for you! Look this way and bend your ear. I am your friendly earth representative for out-of-this-world properties. Oh yes, my acreage is away from the center of gravity, perpendicularly skyward. It is definitely uphill and a paradise of remarkable delights.

It is rich in vegetation, beautification unlimited, panoramic scenery, nature trails, and abundance in everything imaginable. Departure will never be in your vocabulary again. This is a forever homestead.

You'll never meet a stranger here because everyone will know you by your first name! You'll meet the higher echelons of society. It is a friendly, neighborly, cordial place. There are no homeless, no paupers, and you will dine with the common upper class at a banquet table eternally.

The weather is guaranteed 100% sunshine. You can dangle your footsies in the River of Life and pick your favorite fruit from the many, many trees of perpetual fruitage. What a hilltop experience! Do not worry about thorns and thistles. There are none.

It is an ennobling land of enlightenment and knowledge, it is supplied to every occupant. The astonishing headlines of the City Gazette are "No Pain, No Sickness, No Disease Found Here." An extraordinary plateau to invest in. Let me tell you that you would be proud to call this "home."

Turn your television on. There is no bad news to broadcast. This city is crime-free. No ambulances. No hospitals. Doctors and policeman who buy into this are retired.

No burglars, thieves or swindlers. Attorneys are retired, too. No cul-de-sacs, dead-end streets or blind alleys and no maintenance whatsoever.

You might be hesitant to sign up because it sounds unaffordable, but take my word for it, it is easy to write a contract. The Lord God intended His world to fit this description, but a blunder was made. He is anxious to offer restoration and begin again. Listen carefully, my friend, I must warn you. I've seen a lot of sub-divisions in my life, but there is no division here. It is 100% unity.

You may be thinking, "How do I get all this? How do I sign up?" Are you willing to sign a homeowner's covenant? Do not hesitate! This is heavenly real estate offered by Jehovah Properties. He wants to keep the HOA unified. He is top in management, and His Son is in enforcement.

I am just in sales, but I am honored to be affiliated with such credible Superiors. Believe me when I tell you there has never been an opportunity like this. You cannot pass this by. If I can just get you to align your signature right here...

Now, your moving day won't take place until you live your last day on Planet Earth. You will immediately board the Ship of Zion and cross the chilly Jordan River. Then it will happen! Look over yonder! It will be the real estate to die for! Are you ready?

If The Shoe Fits, Wear It

Most people dislike their feet. There is not a good deal of sentiment towards one's feet. Advertisements describe beautiful eyes, attractive smiles, but who boasts of beautiful feet? If you took a survey about what part of the body people think most unattractive, they probably would reply, "my feet!"

An old Persian Proverb says, "I murmured because I had no shoes, until I met a man who had no feet." But God says, "How beautiful on the mountain are the feet of them that bring good news..."
It is interesting to note that one-fourth of all the bones in the body are located in the feet. There are 54 bones, 19 muscles, 100 ligaments and tendons in the feet. The average American walks 70,000 miles in a lifetime or approximately 10 miles a day.

Walking improves blood circulation, clears the mind, and improves the disposition because it circulates blood to the head. Walking cuts tiredness and promotes a reserve of energy for second winds as needed through the day. The oldest book in the Bible, Job, says, "God sees my ways and counts all my steps."

About 80% of Americans suffer from foot pain. The feet can cause distress in the knees, hips, lower back, and even change the posture. It is no wonder when the feet hurt; the entire body agonizes in discomfort.

Let's talk about shoes. I am a shoe peddler and like others with a trade, I have stories. There is a romance about the subject and shoes are not a new vogue.

Abraham in the Book of Genesis spoke of 'laces of the shoes worn by the King of Sodom.' Shoes are used as types and pictures of truths. But do not judge another till you've walked a mile in his shoes.

There are tennis shoes for running a race. They are also known as sneakers, just as Moses sneaked closer to the burning bush. God told him to remove his shoes because he was on holy ground.

There are galoshes, better known as rain boots. It rains on the just and the unjust. Loafers are casual and you can lie down in green pastures. Clogs can be noisy and obnoxious. New expensive shoes may look great, but vanity may overstep comfort with horrid blisters.

Pumps elevate you, but beware pride comes before a fall. The prodigal son was lavished with shoes, a robe and ring when he humbly returned home. The Israelites exited Egypt and spent 40 years in the desert without their shoes wearing out.

There are hiking shoes to climb and move mountains. Army boots are for conquerors and work shoes to put action to your faith, because faith without works is dead.

Then there are big shoes. There is no need to try to fill someone else's shoes. Find what befits you. Need help? There is a heavenly Podiatrist who offers guidance. Whether you wear combat boots or ballerina slippers, if you get your soul right, the soles will be the right footprint in your world.

Miracle Seeds to Bloom Where You Are Planted

Shhh! Com'ere, I've got some classified information to tell you about. I have no idea why this has been concealed for so long. Nevertheless, today I am unveiling the secret of the ages.

How would you like to be able to plant a garden that would bring back over 1,000 times what you planted? You don't need much space to accommodate this planting. If you live in the city without much land, that doesn't matter. If you live in an apartment with only a deck or patio, it will still work. If you're the type that cannot grow anything, just listen to this. These seeds do not grow in dirt. They do not need water or sunshine.

My friend, your mind is a garden. You deliberately plant seeds in the greenhouse of your mind. The seeds are dispersed through your thoughts and broadcast through your words. Pondering and meditating on these seeds of thought causes germination. They are fertilized and cultivated through consideration and repetition. However, if a thought is ignored, it will shrivel up and die.

Eventually thoughts take root. This is marvelous and beyond understanding. The thoughts you sow begin growing in your heart. From the mind to the heart the blossom comes forth directly from the mouth.

And what you sow you shall also reap. Yes, out of the abundance of the heart the mouth speaks. Your words determine your destiny. That's life-changing! You always know what kind of garden is growing inside a person by the burst of words that come forth. Some have a victory garden and others have a cactus garden growing inside.

You have an awesome capacity to plant both anything and everything you choose in order to enhance your life on earth. Your life will be satisfied by the fruit of your mouth. Yes, that's what the Bible says!

May I suggest miracle seeds in variety packages and specialty packs are available, too. Variety packs may include health, wealth, longevity, family, career, and relationships.

The specialty seed packs are of intensity and will help the mind focus on special needed areas. You should welcome the seeds for thought in your internal greenhouse.

In contrast, take caution, as all gardens are threatened by weeds. This inner conservatory is no exception. Weeds with derogatory intentions try to choke the life out of blossoming plants. In retrospect, gutter thoughts may try to crowd out productive thoughts.

Have you heard the expression "Get your mind out of the gutter?" The mind is a traveler and the gutter has broken glass, rodents and stagnant water. You should welcome thoughts to your arboretum where beautiful things can grow. That cannot happen in the gutter.

With the known ability to sow thoughts, you are free to plant whatever you desire in order to receive a harvest in the future. Choose life and everything that pertains to it. Even if the weather is stormy outside, the weather is good for growing inside.

Your mind conservatory is a fertile nursery for growing. Choose your seeds today and I extend a helping hand to you, my friend, to wish you "Happy Planting!"

Sugar and Spice

With This Ring

Marilyn Monroe starred in a movie titled, Diamonds Are A Girl's Best Friend." Why is a diamond so highly favored by the female?

Why is a diamond more significant than an emerald, ruby, or sapphire? That leads to the question, "Why are diamonds used as the sacred token of exchange in matrimony?"

Let's give the diamond some closer scrutiny. Diamonds are the universal symbol of eternal love and commitment, since they are beautiful, strong, and durable as is the tradition of a lasting marriage. It all originated in 1477.

The Archduke Maximillian of Austria gave a diamond ring to Mary of Burgundy. The trend began to give the gem to one's beloved and betrothed.

Romans were the first to wear an engagement ring on the third finger of the left hand.

It is said, there is a vein from the heart, that extends down to this finger and this finger leads straight to the heart. How romantic!

Diamonds are hidden or incognito. That is, they must be unearthed, searched out, and discovered.

They start disguised as a piece of black carbon. Hot lava and tremendous pressure transform that carbon into a diamond. It is the hardest natural material known on earth. A diamond is virtually indestructible. It is also the most transparent material known. It can survive environments that would destroy other materials.

This quality is symbolic of the love relationship bonding the union. True love must be searched for and put to the test for authenticity. There is to be an unbreakable bond between the man and woman.

Transparency is necessary and the wedded bliss should survive any difficulty. But, is a diamond really a girl's best friend?

The circle of the ring represents endless love. No beginning and no end. The diamond is not without tribulation. It is cut, polished, and set.

The more cuts, the more light it reflects. It is placed in a setting of grand design. It has a price tag, most definitely, but to the one it is bestowed, it is priceless.

The man who undertakes to marry also walks through tribulation. The purchase of this significant jewel is not easily wrought. He toils and saves and labors overtime for a long time. In many instances, the diamond is among the largest purchases he has made so far in life.

Undoubtedly, it is a sacrifice, and he has worked hard for this betrothal. The burning flame in his heart is applicable to the inner fire of reflection of the diamond. But is a diamond really a girl's best friend?

He asks for her hand in marriage. What he is really saying is, "Will you be my helpmate? Can you give me a hand?" He is asking her to be available for him, to extend herself to be useful and to aid him. He wants someone to merge with and unite with. In turn, he pledges his responsibility for her, his covering and protection and love.

He embellishes her hand for life with an eternal diamond. But is a diamond really a girl's best friend?

Sometimes animals in the wild and humans conduct courtship in similar ways. A male penguin travels two hundred miles to reach the mating grounds where female penguins breed. He drops a stone in front of one of them, and if she accepts it with a bow, they mate. Same thing in our species.

A man drops a gem in front of a woman and if it appraises to her satisfaction, it is a go! Seriously, is a diamond really a girl's best friend?

The Wedding Charm Bracelet

"Something old, something new, something borrowed, something blue." That was an adage recited during the Victorian era. It was a superstition, but has become a handed down tradition for the bride to be.

She is to collect these items from family and friends to wear on her wedding day.

The "something old" represents continuity. "Something new" depicts optimism for the future. "Something borrowed" symbolizes borrowed happiness and "something blue" stands for purity, love, and fidelity. An added line by the British is "a sixpence in your shoe" and is a wish for good fortune and prosperity. Intended to be given for "something new," I would like to hold a debut for the wedding charm bracelet design. It has ten sanctions as a reminder to the bride to bring rays of sunshine to her marriage.

The eye charm suggests that without a vision the marriage will perish. It will remind her of all the ways she can make her dreams a magnificent obsession. Dreamers have a white hot desire to see their plans materialize. A vision of what a marriage could be if a workable plan is followed, will add ongoing anticipation.

The scroll charm represents a list to self-destruct in 120 seconds. There may be times when a list is needed to total everything a wife has regrets about. All the negatives are disappointing and take their toll. Everyone has thoughts of ending the drama. But what would it do to one's family, children, friends and for the most part, you? Happiness and harmony in marriage are a prerogative. You may bemoan with the list for two minutes, then destroy it.

The heart charm references the love letter of intimacy and heartfelt passion with memoirs of exceptional times. Write a love letter and describe how you feel when he touches you or the pride you have when he has achieved something he aimed for. You may never give the letter to him, but pleasure loving emotions will be cultivated as you write. Open your heart to your most fanciful feelings on paper.

The cupcake charm is to remind you of the sugar content in marriage which is generosity and winsome ways. Give him dessert first.

Dessert is spelled with a double "s", but "desert" only has one "s". People come back for more dessert. But a desert is a wasted barren land that people abandon. You do not want that! "Joy comes in the morning," says Psalm 30:5.

Vibrations released in the morning determine his course for the day. Send him off with a taste of honey in his mouth when he leaves for the day.

Give him sweet words that put harmony in his soul instead of discord. Charm him with gentleness, unselfishness, and consideration.

The fifth charm is a hand. Stroke his dreams. Do not crush them. Eve was made to pleasure Adam. The wife was brought as a bonus to Adam so he would not be comfortless, forsaken, unattended, and uncherished. The stroke could mean a gold strike in the future!

The sixth charm is a mirror. "Mirror, mirror on the wall. Who's the fairest of them all?" Beauty in spirit is what makes a man happy, but efforts to beautify the physical are appreciated too.

The seventh charm is a castle. The man provides the castle, but it is not complete without a queen. Most men want money more than any other thing, but they often want it to please the woman of their choice. Let the king know often that you appreciate what he has provided.

In the Garden of Eden, Eve wanted more and more, until she got us all into trouble. Be grateful for your privileges and blessings, and let him know often.

The eighth charm is a plus sign. Women have a need to increase and develop their interior selves. Cultivate industriousness. A virtuous woman may deal in real estate, be creative with her hands, and have a keen eye for multiplying assets for the family. Remember, your achievements add value to him too.

The ninth charm is a rubber band. Have elasticity of soul. Be willing to adapt to temporary situations. Bend a knee to problem areas and extend yourself when needed. Even this will pass!

The tenth and final charm is a ring. The circle symbolizes unending love. Salvage something from every setback. Do not waste time thinking, "If only I had..." You have been gathering experience and understanding so do not spend time and energy lamenting the past. Learn what your husband does not like. Do not obstruct the eternal unending circle of love.

Now with a strong mind, a fixed attitude and the favor of God, take your wedded husband, cherish him and pledge your loyalty to him. Love, honor, comfort, and keep him in health and in sickness, in prosperity and adversity, as long as you both shall live!

The Best Thing Men Have Going For Them

A woman is a man's passion, the object of his wealth, the heartbeat of his home, and his child's touchstone. A woman is a man's treasure. In his opinion, she does not decrease when she leans on him for support. He is championed by the very idea.

She is the king's challenge and the nation's conquest. When women are elevated, the whole nation begins to thrive.

Thus, the woman dictates the heroes of the land, herself being a heroine. Women are the world's pacesetters. All creation bows to their whims.

Women are an arrangement of fruitfulness. Even God referred to them as "the fruitful vine." They hold the deed to acres of emotion. They are, by nature, productive. Their harvest is not always a predictable gain, however. Their emotions are as uncertain as the weather. They are apprehensive about the future, but always planning-and always worrying.

They are in themselves a testimonial of a complex nature. They can be women of ill repute or of career caliber. They can move with the spirit of a single or blend with a corporate body. They can have a clean streak or be a moody monthly. They can have a dishwater disposition or the tone of a fairytale princess. They can possess the temper of a panther or the softness of a kitten. A woman is her own representative.

Women are distinguished by so much more than belonging to the female gender, and more than being the mother of men. A true feminist is ladylike, tender, sensitive, and a well of wonderful emotion.

When women relinquish those virtues, they cease to be a first-rate female. Those qualities associated with femininity are the very essentials men need to promote their masculinity!

Women are, indeed, the perfector of manhood. They are the object of a man's obsession for living. They are the best thing men have going for them!

Betty's Bread Kitchen

Betty's Bread Kitchen

Hey you! You better not be doing what I think you are doing! You would not be ripping the cherished crust from my bread, would you? Can you even imagine how, in the wee hours of the morning, I was going strong; toiling, kneading, rolling, to produce this prized loaf of gold? And you are removing the beautiful brown etherealness? What a hoecake!

I don't know what this world is coming to. The celestial loaf is not appreciated like it used to be. Travel to almost any country and sit in any restaurant and they'll serve you bread. If the poor have nothing, they have bread. If the rich have everything, they still have bread.

But listen, Johnny Cake, it is the glory of my kitchen and the finest sustenance offered on my menu. No Sourdough Joe leaves a crumb or piece of crust on their plate in my restaurant. No siree. I'm offended, Cornbread! I guess you expect to get some reduced price 'cause you didn't eat it all? "Breaking bread" doesn't mean tearing off what you don't like!

I bet you are one of those people who, when you were a kid, would whine, "I don't like the crust!" or "I hate onions!" or "I don't like my food to touch each other on the plate!" You thought you were a little dumplin', but you were a brat! 'Should've shipped you off to Africa where the children are starving.

They would have given anything for just a morsel from Betty's Bread Kitchen.

No country claims to be the exclusive source of bread. Of course, Betty's Bread Kitchen holds the Bonne bouche (French for chef's special) for the not-to-be-improved-upon perfect golden crusted loaf a la carte.

You can get a tortilla in Mexico or a bagel in New York, and I know bread is available everywhere, but Pumpernickel, you have come to the right place for fineness. My bread is served in many delightful ways.

It is toasted, jellied, buttered, flattened and grilled. It can be a sandwich, sweet roll, hot dog bun, croissant, or dinner roll. And this is the right place for unequivocal satisfaction for the taste buds. Any scone should know that!

I am very pleased with myself and it just goes to show folks why I have an enviable self-respect. I do not have false modesty, because I serve an imposing loaf. But I the willing, led by the unknowing, am doing the impossible for the ungrateful.

I have done so much for so long with so little, I am now qualified to do anything with nothing! Furthermore, I do get ticked at the wastefulness and bad manners of some of my patrons. Apologies!

Now I would not want anyone to walk out of here without me telling them what is needed beyond my precious sustenance. There is the famous "Bread of Life." What bread is to hunger, Jesus is to the soul.

He is known as the "Bread of Life." Your stomach may feel empty, but your soul hungers, too. It would be advantageous for you to accept an invitation from the One who is ultimately internal and universal.

He will not interrupt your life, but will infill you with the proper ingredients for abundant life. Some people say, "Do not fill up on bread. Save room for the entrée." I say, "Try a slice of Betty's loaf and the 'Bread of Life' can be your main course." In fact, He is the Way, the Truth, and the Life.

The Hungry Hobo

An old man came wandering into my famed "Betty's Bread Kitchen" late one afternoon. After giving him the once over and wishing he had taken time to clean up a little, I asked, "Can I help you?"
"I just want a slice of bread."

"Well, of course. You have come to the right place!" Under the counter I stored a cookbook with many of my favorite recipes loved by my customers. I read a few to him, and then recited some of the rich ingredients used to bake my coveted loaves.

I told him all about the need for grain and barley, whole wheat and cracked wheat. I even gave him some of my exact measurements to impress him. I wanted him to know that I knew precisely what I was talking about!

"I'm hungry. I know your bread is good. They told me about it on skid row."

The vagrant surprised me, admitting where he came from. "Why, yes, just follow me and we will see about that delicious bread I bake!" He hobbled behind me, not muttering a word.

The hallowed halls were decorated with artful framed representations of the tasteful breads we serve. I paused to emphasize the many rooms where preparation takes place and the commercial ovens used in baking the incomparable loaves.

"Our facilities are a cut above the competition, the wanna-be-rivals. You see, our "baker's dozen" is of notable diversity. You name it. We have it!" He stumbled a bit, but followed me.

"This room is most impressive," I pointed out. This is our employee chapel. Notice the stained-glass windows!" The vagrant did not say a word. "People come from everywhere to our gatherings here, and of course, we offer complimentary bread upon their departure.

They support our efforts and like to hear the talks I give every Friday from the cookbook of life."
The freeloader was now seated on the front row. "I'm hungry. I just want some bread," he murmured.

"Yes! Yes! We will finish our tour after I show you one more thing." He tottered behind me as we approached the front door.

I opened it and said, "Look! Do you see other restaurants on this street? Of course, they make their claims, but they do not bake bread like "Betty's." Some of them use too much shortening, and others turn their ovens too high.

But my bread is just right and the envy of the trade. There is a secret ingredient to my successful recipe which I choose not to reveal. But I assure you; I am a connoisseur and align myself to the book."

The bum turned to walk away. "Hey! Don't you want some bread?" I raised my voice. He stopped, looked back at me, and shrugged his shoulders. "I lost my appetite, lady."
I turned and headed for my office to work on Friday's talk. It is titled "Life Without Jesus Is Like A Donut There's A Hole In The Middle Of Your Heart!"

I thought to myself, "I was getting to that, Mr. Ragamuffin. I was gonna tell you all about it. There is help for all you ne'er-do-wells. You just got impatient!"

My, my, people can be a pain! By the way, pain is French for "bread." Don't you just love it? People just don't appreciate what I try to do for 'em, anyway!

Everything You Ever Wanted To Know About Bread
(But Were Afraid To Ask!)

I admit I am a bread-aholic. What do you expect from the proprietor of Betty's Bread Kitchen? The trade of the baker is one of the oldest crafts in the world. I am honored to be numbered among them. It is no passing trend.

Bread has been around a long time - 30,000 years some say. Loaves and rolls have been found in ancient Egyptian tombs. In the British Museum's Egyptian galleries, you can see actual loaves baked over five thousand years ago! The ability to sow and reap cereal grains may be one of the chief causes which led man to dwell in communities rather than wandering, hunting, and herding cattle.

Throughout much of history a person's social station could be discerned by the color of bread they consumed. For generations white bread was the preferred bread of the rich, while the poor ate whole grain or "black bread." This was because whiter flours were more expensive; however, this notion reversed in the late 20th century.

Whole grain became the preference as having superior nutritional value while white bread became associated with lower class ignorance of nutrition. With a growing variety of foods, bread remains important to our diet and is a complete life-sustainer. Old wives' tales suggest the bread crust makes a person's hair curlier. The first and last slices of a loaf are sometimes referred to as the heel or the crust. The crust is rumored to be healthier than the rest of the loaf.

Studies reveal the crust has more dietary fiber and antioxidants, notably pronyl-lysine. This is being researched for its potential colorectal cancer inhibitory properties.

Bread has a prominent place in our local market, our cupboards, and even in our language. The word "bread" or "dough" is a slang for money. Our work is our "bread and butter."

The "breadwinner" is the household's main contributor. The "breadbasket" is an agriculturally productive region. "Breaking bread" is togetherness in communion or fellowship. The Lord's Prayer says, "Give us this day our daily bread." It is known as "the staff of life." Jesus, the "Bread of Life," was born in Bethlehem which means, "House of Bread." Interesting, don't you think?

Do you know which side your bread is buttered on? Better remember to say, "Thank You!" And always be reminded to "cast your bread upon the waters" and your generosity will be returned to you. Just a little food for thought and something to chew on!

Seymour By The Seashore

What Difference Does It Make?

At the peak of the tourist season, a man stood at the seashore, eyes squinting from the sun and sand between his toes. He was observing what appeared to be beach madness. He watched the itching palms and tight fists of the eager indulgence of beachcombers to gather all the shells they could.

They would outdo each other with fine specimens of hermit crabs, starfish, sea urchins, sand dollars, and sea snails. They were proud of their collections and anxious to show friends back home what they had swooped up.

It is not uncommon at the seashore to see people with a collector's morality. They are the people who are trying to collect life and own a piece of happiness. They are the consumers, availing themselves of the living beauty of the coastline.

I noticed a middle-aged man who stooped over, then stood up to hurl an object out to sea. He was bronze and I could tell he was no newcomer to the shore. I couldn't imagine what he was throwing into the water. I walked over to initiate a conversation with him.

"What are you doing?" I asked with sincere curiosity.

"I am a star thrower," the man replied.

I expected to see a sand dollar or perhaps a flat rock with a frisbee shape, but not so. He picked up a starfish and spun it out into the sea.

"It may live," he said, "if the offshore pull is strong enough."

"What difference does it make? There are so

many starfish around here. Everyone else is collecting them and taking them back home. You are the first one I've ever seen that is trying to rescue them."

"My friend," the man expounded, "life cannot be collected. Happiness is not a destination, cannot be owned, earned, worn, or consumed. Happiness is the wonderful experience of living every minute with love, grace, and gratitude. The gift of life is not a treasure hunt.

You asked 'what difference does it make if I throw a star fish back into the sea?' It makes a difference to the fish. It makes all the difference in the world. That fish might be able to go on living. And I have turned its life from a collection to a celebration."

Maybe we should observe and commemorate life each day, marking a red letter on the calendar meaning, "This is the day the Lord has made. Let us rejoice and be glad in it." The multitude musters and horde their collection and possessions, but the celebrator hallows life and commemorates what is important.

The Sand Dollar

The sand dollar, by all appearance, seems to have netted the thumbprint of God! The seashell's story has been classified as a legend. A legend is an improbable, traditional story, also known as a myth or folk tale. The story has the resemblance of this definition, but is dissimilar to a legend and more than distinct in nature. It is an absolute marvel.

The sea has given us the lowly sand dollar and its impressions reveal a phenomenal story. It exhibits the visual markings of the Christmas story, the crucifixion of Christ, and the Easter story.

On one side of the sand dollar shell is the perfectly etched poinsettia, known as "The flower of the Holy Night." It is said the poinsettia, once a white bloom, took on crimson red after Christ's death. Remarkably, the Bethlehem Star is impressed in the center of the poinsettia on each sand dollar.

The Easter lily is etched beautifully on the reverse side of the sand dollar. Its petals are shaped like trumpets to proclaim Christ's victorious resurrection from the tomb.

There are four holes plus one on each shell. The four holes reveal the nail- pierced hands and feet of Christ on the cross. The fifth hole reminds us of the wound on His side from the Roman soldier's spear.

Surprise! Now shake the shell and if you break it, there are five little white doves inside, perfectly shaped and separate. No matter how small the shell, the five doves reside. Jesus left this earth and promised to send the Holy Spirit, Who is symbolized as a dove. The Holy Spirit would do five things: comfort, guide, teach, put you in remembrance, and point the world to God's Son. Five doves-five mandates!

The size of the sand dollar does not reduce the message. Even a tiny shell bears the markings that tell this story. "Even a child is known by his doings whether they be pure or right." Proverbs 20:11

Several times I have picked these shells from the beach and even purchased more perfect ones in gift shops. I am intrigued by the consistent perfection of their imprints. They all make known the same story.

Not saying a word, they communicate the wondrous episode of John 3:16, "For God so loved the world that He gave His only begotten Son that whosoever believes on Him should not perish but have everlasting life."

The shell is extraordinary and it is mysterious. Or is it? "For since the creation of the world, God's invisible qualities...His eternal power and divine nature have been clearly seen, being understood from what has been made, so that men are without excuse." Romans 1:20.

The sand dollar is an astonishing piece of God's handiwork.

The Seashore Antidote

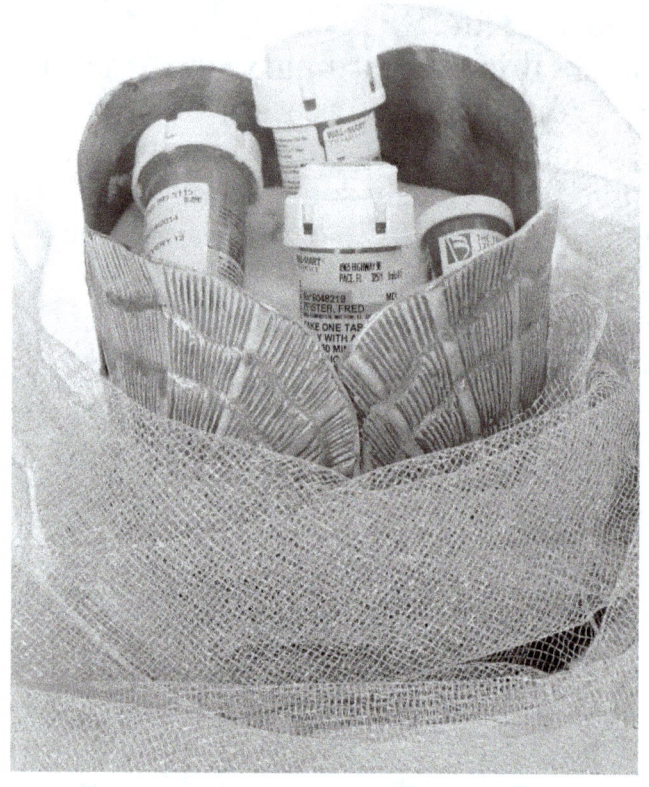

A man had become so despondent that hopelessness closed in on every meaningful part of his life. His will, his work, even his family were so reduced in his mind, darkness weighed him down from morning till night.

Finally in the depth of his depression, he went to see his old friend, the family doctor. The doctor listened to him talk about his problems, saw his gloom, and then asked him, "When you were a young boy, what did you like to do best?"

The man answered, "I liked to go to the seashore."

"All right," the doctor said. "I have the perfect treatment for you.   Listen carefully to my instructions.   Tomorrow I want you to spend all day at the shore.   Find a place on the beach where you are all alone and spend the entire day there from 9:00 in the morning until 6:00 in the evening.   Do not be distracted in any way, and take nothing to read or listen to.

I am going to give you four prescriptions, and you must take them in order.   Take the first one at 9:00, the second one at noon, the third at 3:00 and the last one at 6:00.   Do not look at them now, but wait until you arrive at the shore tomorrow morning.

The man agreed to take the doctor's advice. The next morning just before 9:00, he parked his car in a desolate area on the seashore.   The wind blew in from the sea and the surf was high and pounding.   He walked to a sand dune near the bubbling surf and sat down.

He took out Prescription #1, opened it, and read it.   It read, "Listen." That was all that was written on it.   The one word, "Listen."   For the next three hours that is all he did.   He listened to the powerful winds and the seagulls' cries.   The surf beat the shore.   He sat quietly and he listened.

At noon he took out the second prescription and read it.   It said, "Reminisce."   For the next three hours he thought of the many events in his life that had caused him this heaviness.   He thought of the struggles and the successes.   He also thought of happy times, and he smiled.

At 3:00 he tore open the third prescription. It said "Review your motives." This took his exclusive attention and focus, and so the remaining time moved quickly by. For three hours he re-emerged into the past. He thought about his reason for living. He re-examined his intent for the future.

At 6:00 with nightfall moving in, and a fine salt mist in the air, he read the fourth and final prescription. It read, "Scrawl your worries in the sand." He paused and thought. Yes, there was a particular problem, that came to his mind and it had been dominating his thought life recently.

He walked to the hard sand and with a stick he wrote that problem in the sand. He stood for a moment looking at it. Then he turned and walked back to his car.

The restless rolling tide had already washed the worry away. He got in his car and drove homeward. If the man had gone to the Great Physician, he would have been advised to,

"Take no thought for the morrow; for the morrow shall take thought for the things of itself...Take no thought saying, 'What shall we eat? Or what shall we drink? Or wherewithal shall we be clothed? For your heavenly Father knows that you have need of these things. But seek first the Kingdom of God, and His righteousness; and all these things shall be added unto you." Matthew 6:31

Mullygrubs

In The Mullygrubs

Oh my aching back! I would give my right arm for some relief. Don't you hate it when pain is killing you? It's gonna get worse. I just know it. I can't see no hope for the future at all. It's hard to be able to bear an injury. But then again, to have a grievance is to have a purpose in life. Just what I need! Oh well, every path has a puddle. The bed is too short to stretch out; the blanket too narrow to wrap around me. The worrywart medicine just got thrown out. Humbug! I'm bothered.

News can only be bad. Fights can only be lost. I can only get more unlucky. It's too late. It's no use. What strength do I have that I should continue to hope? Since I can't help myself, the hope of success has been banished from me. Who has enough credit in this world to pay for his miseries? Be done with it. Flibbertigibbet!

Looks like the day is turnin' grey. Grey is a color that always seems on the eve of changin' to some other color. It'll be dark soon. I like the color black. At nighttime brainless people are less visible. They retire for the night. Life is one long process of getting tired.

None of us can help the things life has done to us. They're done before you realize it, and once they're done they make you do other things until at last everything comes between you and what you'd like to be, and you've lost your true self forever.

I'm just disappointed in what life's done to me. The tragedy of life is not that man loses, but that he almost wins.

Some people are just downright lucky. But me, if I didn't have bad luck, I'd have no luck at all. But then again, to be without the things you want is an indispensable part of happiness.

Sometimes I just feel like gettin' on my head and garglin' peanut butter. I want to yell "Look at me! Notice anything different?" Nobody pays any attention unless you give them somethin'. I have nothin' to give. I'm so poor I can't even pay attention. I don't care about the unkind things people say about me so long as they don't say 'em to my face.

There's is so much good in the worst of us, and so much bad in the best of us, that it hardly behooves any of us to talk about the rest of us. Lord save us all from old age and broken health and a hope tree that has lost the faculty of puttin' out blossoms. There are two tragedies in life; one is to lose your heart's desire, and the other is to gain it. But what counts is not necessarily the size of the dog in the fight—it's the size of the fight in the dog. Fellows like me, though, we lost most our teeth a long time ago.

"All of us who have become like one who is unclean, and all our righteous acts are like filthy rags; we all shrivel up like a leaf, and like the wind our sins sweep us away." Isaiah 64:6

Got Grub?

This joint looks like Mother Hubbard's cupboard. There ain't nothin' to eat round here. When a man's stomach is full, makes no difference whether he's rich or poor, 'cause he's just satisfied. But the belly is ungrateful. It always forgets I already gave it somethin'. What am I cravin'? A good meal oughta begin with hunger. You can eat garbage provided you sprinkle it liberally with ketchup, mustard, chili sauce, Tabasco sauce, cayenne pepper and any other condiments that destroy the original flavor of the dish. And small amounts of poison are added to improve the food's appearance and delay its putrefaction.

French fries! The French fried potato has become an inescapable horror in most every public eatin' place. "French fries" says the menu, but they're not French fries no more. They are a furry textured substance with the taste of plastic wood. Drats! And cheeseburgers? Cheese is milk's leap toward immortality.

Tell me what you eat and I'll tell you who you are. One thing's for sure, an appetite is a solution to the labor question. When you find someone who's not doin' a good job, you can go figure they're not hungry. A man seldom thinks with more seriousness of nothin' than he does of his dinner.

The important thing is to pull yourself up by your own hair, turn yourself inside out, and see the world with ravenous eyes. That's what I do.

I look through my army-green tinted glasses every day, not rose colored.

Then a good dinner and feastin' reconciles everybody. All eatin' is a kind of dogmatizing-the eater's way of lookin' at things is better than the eatee's. Man is the only animal that can remain on friendly terms with the victims he tends to eat until he eats them. Listen to me now. A single conversation across the table with a wise man like me is better than ten years mere study of books.

Dinner lubricates business too. A man and his meal are the day's meditation. The preacher said the other day, "He that has a merry heart has a continual feast." (Proverbs 15:15) I been thinkin' 'bout that and I reckon that's my answer! The reason I can't get satisfied with nothin' I eat, is melancholy me. I lie down with my dogs and get up with fleas. My house eats onions together.

That's the only harmony we have under our roof. For the time bein', we're separate from the world and who cares anyhow, as long as we got grub.

Mully Meets Molly

I was havin' a man to man meetin' of the heart with Uncle Willy. He said, "Mully, don't you think it is 'bout time you find a real pretty little damsel and make yourself a nice match?" I got kinda choked up and emotional cause he'd never talked that kinda talk to me before. "Well, Uncle Will, funny you would bring that up to me, 'cause I was just thinkin' about that neighbor girl, Molly. But I know I was hallucinatin' 'cause she probably wouldn't even give a peep at an ole dog like me.

Besides, what would I talk to her about? The rats in the cellar are overtakin' our dump? Or would you like to come over to my flea trap? Aw, it's always somethin', ain't it, Uncle Will? And if it's gonna happen, it'll happen to me. What I mean is bein' footloose. You know—solo. Nobody would ever have me."

"Boy, anybody who is any good is different from anybody else. I'm thinkin' it's the right time to give you some kinship advice 'bout the opposite sex. Now you listen loud and clear from an oldster who knows the reins. Women are quite unlike our breed. They have higher voices, longer hair, smaller waistlines, daintier feet and prettier hands. They also have the habit of using the upper hand. Now a woman's feller should be taller, older, heavier, uglier and hoarser than she is. A man should choose a wife by his ear, not his eye." Uncle Willy gave me a mouthful of counsel.

"How many of these women can a man have?" I asked.

"Sixteen!" Uncle Willy quickly answered.

"Sixteen wives? How do you figure?" I was flabbergasted at his answer.

"Four better, four worse, four richer, and four poorer. That's what I heared the bishop say in the last weddin' I went to," said the wise old gaffer.

"I know you got wisdom, Uncle Willy, but I think you're off kilter on that deduction. That's not even lawful!" I had to rebut him a little there.

"In marriage, be wise, prefer the person before the money, virtue before the beauty, the mind before the body; then you have a wife, a friend, a companion, a second self. And always remember, women like silent men. They think they're listenin'." That was no morsel coming from my uncle.

After digestin' all that schoolin' I decided to go over and meet Molly. I made us strangers acquainted, and for a first acquaintance, it went pretty good, I thought.

I gave her a first taste of my gender wisdom like I was learnin' from Uncle Willy. I said, "The greatest love is a mother's; then comes a dog's; and then comes a sweetheart." Then I asked her to be my valentine.

"*Valentine?*" she questioned. "*As in February? I'm dumbfounded.*"

I knew that would happen! She came right out and told me she'd just found dumb. I asked myself the question, would true love find me? Not a nitwit like me. What a blockhead. I could've told you before it happened.

Now all my days I'll be Hee Hawin "Gloom, despair and agony on me. It's deep dark depression and excessive misery. If it weren't for bad luck, I'd have no luck at all."

One of these days is none of these days. Life is one long postponement.

Nannette The Nanny

Heaven's Pediatrician Knows

What is the resemblance between kids and olive plants? What an interesting comparison. Can you guess who made the parallelism? It was God when He said, "Your children will be like olive plants around your table." Psalm 128:3 Olive trees are among the most difficult trees on earth to grow and become fruit bearing.

They require a lot of special care and handling. You are right on, Doctor! My childcare experience has brought me to this deduction: it is one of the most difficult tasks on earth.

Olive trees produce fruit early at four or five years old. Other fruit trees may not bear fruit for seven or eight years. "Even a child is known by his actions, by whether his conduct is pure and right." Proverbs 20:11.

There is a pit inside that must be removed before an olive can be enjoyed. There is a carnal, defiant nature in every newborn, too. That adorable cooing baby soon resists authority and discipline with a, "No!" Did the mother show that toddler how to throw a tantrum? I don't think so. Teaching and guidance begin before the first words or first steps. Olives have alternate fruit bearing seasons--every other year; sometimes there is no fruit.

Children have seasons or stages of growth likewise. I know all about the "terrible two's," followed by childhood, youth, adolescence, and eventually adulthood. A baby is an angel whose wings decrease as his legs increase.

Olives have a bitterness which requires five

dippings in sodium peroxide (lye). Therefore, they cannot be picked for instant enjoyment as apples, pears, or peaches. All fruit is bitter before it ripens. I have witnessed teens that have been through a few dipping's, and still need more.

Handpicking is required in harvest because the fruit bruises easily. The tree is shaken gently. Spanking and discipline are also part of the agenda in raising productive children. Take it easy, though. They are little people. Their torn jacket is soon mended; but hard words bruise the heart of a child.

The olive fly can damage the bark, leaves, and fruit to the extent the tree is corrupted and may die. The name of the enemy of God is Beelzebub and it means "Lord of the flies." What an implication in child rearing. The devil don't raise no good kids.

You may not be able to read between the lines, but as a nanny, I find it engaging. "It is no hard matter to get children, but after they are born, then begins the trouble, solicitude and care rightly to train, principle, and bring them up," said Montaigne. Children are the anchors that hold a mother's life. I will always have a job.

Give Notice

A former Miss America told of how her dreams were nurtured and cultivated at age five. Her father owned a little country store. The milk man delivered fresh milk in sterilized glass bottles daily. She looked forward to his arrival because he always greeted her with, "How's my little Miss America today?"

Robert Schuller of the Crystal Cathedral in Garden Grove, California had a visit from his uncle on their Iowa farm when he was seven. His uncle said one day, "Well Robert, I guess you're going to be a preacher, eh?" Little Robert turned and looked up to the sky and prayed quietly, "And God, make me a good one!" For decades, Dr. Schuller has affected the world with his possibility-thinking message in books and Sunday morning television programs.

I was a nanny for a little boy who used to look up and say, "When I grow up I want to be a Hostess cupcake semi-driver." As children develop, they think big and have lifetime dreams. Familiar voices often say, "How are you going to do that? How will you have enough money? That's an impossible dream!"

By the time they have reached adulthood and are able to pursue their goals, they've been brainwashed by negative influences. They ask, "What's the use?" or say, "I could never do that!" They need assurance, a stamp of approval, and a confidence boost in order to believe in themselves. Perhaps a child who is fussed over gets a feeling of destiny, and he thinks he is in the world for something important.

These days I watch a lady bring her pet regularly to the dog park. She lauds over that furry Fido. She cheers him and assures him he is a good dog. "Atta boy!" "Good boy!" She positively reinforces his obedience. The big black dog struts and wags steadily. His master has convinced him he is the Best of Show in Westminster Abbey.

Jean Anthelme Brillat-Savarin said, "To invite someone into your house is to take charge of their happiness for as long as they're under your roof." Did children ask to be born? Are they not a recipient of the parent's bounty? Should they not be lavished with acceptance and endowed with compliments, advanced with training and improvement as they develop? Listen to them. What notions are they conceiving? What castles are they building?

A balloon salesman was releasing colorful balloons on the streets of New York City. He alternated the colors with yellow, red and white. A little boy asked him if a black balloon would go up in the clouds like the bright colors did. The man told him it is what's inside the balloons that make them go up. Do you know what's inside the children in your home?

A man brought his three daughters to my house. They were three, five and seven years of age. They were dressed in pretty dresses and looked adorable. To my surprise he introduced them like this: "This is the one who won't eat, this is the one who won't mind her mother, and this is the one who cries all the time." He was giving them something to live down. We reap what we sow, as well as what we sow into other's minds.

The way we see children largely determines how they react.

Take a bar of iron and use it for a door stop and it is worth a dollar. Manufacture horseshoes from that iron and they're worth about fifty dollars. Take the same bar of iron, remove the impurities, refine it into steel and manufacture it into mainsprings for precision watches. Now it is worth a quarter of a million dollars.

The way we see the bar of iron makes the difference, and the way we see little people and their future makes a difference. We are a mirror to them, and they look into that mirror for self-approval. As a nanny, I understand I am that child's green light. I can be a deterrent to their world, or I can give them the "go ahead!"

Straighten Up and Talk Right!

I am revisiting the olive grove, if you will overlook my repetition of Psalm 128:3, "Your children will be like olive plants round about your table." It is time to be straightforward on the subject of discipline. The Creator has some infinite parental wisdom with His analogy of children and olive plants, (along with horses and ships).

The olive tree has a gnarled trunk that puzzles me. Normally a crooked or bent tree can be re-staked and trained to grow straight. Not so with this fruit tree. The many trunks wrap around each other and grow in every direction.

A grove farmer could re-stake the tree time and again, but the trunk will grow its own way. The grower understands this twisted tangled perplexity and does not regard it as troublesome.

Children often have a different agenda than the parents planned. The mother or father may have ambitions and secret dreams for their children and they try to curb this unusual tangled growth. "Train up a child in the way he should go and when he is old he will not depart from that way." Proverbs 22:6. "In the way he should go" literally means "In keeping with his way," not necessarily the way the parents think he should go. "The child's way" may refer to his temperament, bent and inborn characteristics.

The tree cannot be re-staked, but it can grow to be an imposing, grand, and overwhelming fruitful tree. Children can take us by surprise too, with inventiveness, aptitudes, gifts, and even genius.

The Hebrew word for "train" relates to the inside of the mouth, the gums, the palate, or the roof of the mouth. "When we put bits into the mouths of horses to make them obey us, we can turn the whole animal. Or take ships as an example. Although they are large and are driven by strong winds, they are steered by a small rudder wherever the pilot wants to go.

Likewise, the tongue is a small part of the body, but it makes great boasts. Consider that a great forest is set on fire by a small spark. The tongue also is a fire, a world of evil among the parts of the body.

It corrupts the whole person, sets the whole course of his life on fire." James 3:3-6

"The tongue has the power of life and death and those who love it will eat its fruit." Proverbs 18:21. There are eight hundred thousand words in the English language. The average person knows about ten thousand and uses five thousand in everyday speech.

There is enormous power here: the power to heal or wound, to encourage or dishearten, to speak truth or to deceive, to praise or to criticize. In my duties as a nanny, I have diversity, but teaching children to talk right is my most crucial task.

I am impressing their world by teaching vocabulary. If I can teach them to talk right, they will eventually live right. Those tangled trunks will grow taller.

We play a vocal game. Spending those five thousand words, we find the entire grandeur glossary and go back and forth with each other till we run out of words. We use units of expression like magnificent, wonderful, victorious, charming, laughing, joyous, sunshine, appreciate, and preparation. Someday they will have a fabulous vocabulary and will have mastered the art of positive communication.

Words can be wonderful and winning. Dennis the Menace was all dressed up in his magician's suit but said he could only do two magic tricks because he knew only two magic words, "Please" and "Thank You." The child who is taught to say "Thank You" is taught one of the most important qualities— gratitude.

The little boy or girl who is taught "Please" is learning a mannerly way of asking for favor. It is a foundation for winning friends and influencing people.

If I can teach them to talk right, they will walk right, and they will climb every mountain!

Dr. Livelonger

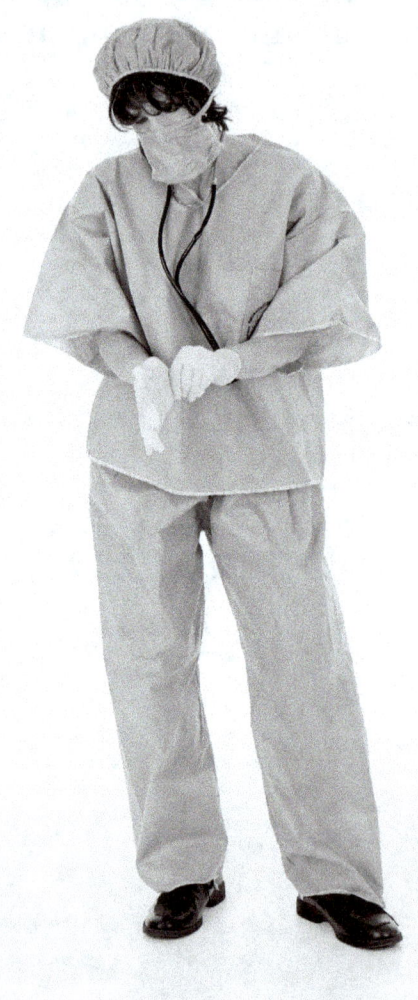

Peer Into A Perfect Work

Before the atomic age, professors used to say that a person's worth, from a strictly chemical standpoint, was about thirty-two dollars on the going market. In recent years, scientists now calculate that if the electronic energy in the hydrogen atoms of your body could be utilized, you could supply all the electrical needs of a large, highly industrialized country for nearly a week.

A DuPont scientist said that the atoms of your body contain a potential energy of more than eleven million kilowatts per pound. By this estimate, the average person is worth about eighty-five billion dollars.

Moreover, the electrons in the atoms of your body are not just particles of matter; they are waves of living energy. And these waves ripple out and spread themselves in patterns of light, and as they move, they sing!

If you had the proper hearing aid, you could hear a great flow merging with the waves of neighboring atoms.

Not only do they sing, they shine! If you would stand in front of an infrared television camera in a completely dark room, the screen would show you, from top to toe, as a glistening, radiating, gleaming form.

Since the beginning of time, never has there been another with your mind, your heart, your eyes, your ears, your hands, your hair, and your mouth. None that came before, none that live today and none that come tomorrow can walk and talk and move and think exactly like you. You are different from all others. You are a unique creature.

None can duplicate your brush strokes, none can make your chisel marks, none can facsimile your handwriting, none can produce your child, and in truth, none has the ability to perform exactly like you. Henceforth, capitalize on this difference, for it is an asset to be promoted to the fullest.

You are nature's greatest miracle. No beast, no plant, no wind, no rain, no rock, no lake had the same beginning as you, for you were conceived in love and brought forth with a purpose. "For I know the plans I have for you," declares the Lord, "plans to prosper and not to harm you, plans to give you hope and a future." Jeremiah 29:11

My co-worker maintains a high degree of excellence and supreme knowledge, and is crowned with impeccability. It is my pleasure and an honor to work hand to hand with such a peerless ally; He is never taken unaware. Together we are in this undertaking for life.

The plaque on the office door reads, *"Jehovah"* and my name is below it, *"Dr. Livelonger."*

Life Is Good

A man was watching a television show and his five-year-old son kept interrupting. Finally, the man tore a page from the newspaper. It was a large picture of the world, and he tore it into a dozen pieces and gave it to his son.

He said, "Here, put this picture together with this tape and let's see how long it takes you." Then he continued to watch his program.

In a surprisingly short time the boy had the picture all taped together. The father looked and said, "Amazing! How did you do that so fast?"

The little boy said, "There was a picture of a man on the other side. I just put the man together, and then the world was all together." "That's right, son," the father said, "When the man is all together, his world is all together, too."

"How good is man's life, the mere living!
How fit to employ all the heart and the soul and
the senses forever in joy! "
                         Robert Browning (1855)

I may have days in which I am depressed or confused, but I remember this: do my work. Not just my work and no more, but more for the lavishing's sake. Put my heart into it and the sky will clear. That I exist is a perpetual surprise! I decided for what purpose I was placed on this earth. I am breathing, my heart is beating, and this is reason to resolve I am a contributor in life today. Perhaps I am a contributor to your life. I am a created masterpiece. I am not the first to be born, nor the last, but a current participator. On assignment to meet me are my needs supplied. I'm not a random idea on earth, but a deliberate conception formed with purpose, on purpose.

I decided to take courage and live strong. I am not "almost," or "on the brink" and will never say, "If only". I decided to be a helper and not a hinderer—a developer and not a destroyer. I'm breaking through, not breaking down.

There is greater tendency to laugh than to cry. It has been said, "He only is rich who owns the day." The Lord has made this day. I will rejoice and be glad in it.

This day is working for me! How am I faring? Well, thank you. Well favored, well maintained, encouraged in my heart, which is a wellspring of life. My circumstances are not my status. The world is making room for me today and I'm not willing to stop for I've only just begun.

I'm endowed with an awe-inspiring power—the power to choose. My choices are the magnet that attract good things to me. I decided to choose life and all that pertains to it. And the world is my beneficiary.

'Life consists of what a man is thinking all day.'
Emerson

Accept the Exceptional

Your body is the most gloriously accurate instrument in this universe. Given the preferred fuel, pure air, exercise, sunshine and keeping it internally clean with a healthy diet; your body will last indefinitely and function perfectly. A healthy body is an efficient chemical factory. Supplemented with the correct raw materials, it should be capable of developing strong tissue and good resistance against most bacteria, viruses and other environmental impacts.

The only fine machine I know, that contains its own repair shop that can work wonders if you give it the proper tools. It is constantly working for you. Its cells are being destroyed and renewed every second. Biologically, it has no age limit. Every cell in your body is renewed within eleven months.

You have the capacity between your ears to store more information than can be reserved in dozens of man's most sophisticated computers. In your very own mind you can amass more information than the millions of volumes in the Library of Congress.

Scientists tell us that if man were to attempt to create a human brain, it would cost billions of dollars, would be larger than the Empire State Building and would require more electricity than a city of thousands. Its construction would involve the most brilliant men in the world.

Yet with all of this size, cost, and power requirements, this man-made brain couldn't originate a single thought, which you can do in the blink of an eye.

Your remarkable mind brings seventy-two muscles into perfect coordination each time you utter a word.

But to what end or for what purpose is man? He can be killed by a leopard one-fourth of his weight or by a germ or virus that's totally invisible. He has no protective coloring at all. He can be easily seen in any kind of environment.

He cannot run fast enough to escape any animal bent on catching him. He cannot swim very far and he has no claws or sharp teeth and can hardly climb a tree. His vision is weak, and he cannot even catch a puppy that doesn't want to be caught.

Nevertheless, you are exceptional because you were given the greatest gift of all: Reason. You can think. Because you can think, you do not blend in with your environment—you change your locality to match you!

In fact, just as you can tell what country an animal came from by looking at the pattern of its coloring, you can tell how a person is reasoning by observing their surroundings. Habitat fits the person just as an animal fits the environment.

To the exact extent a person uses the greatest gift on earth, the gift of reasoning, will determine the kind of entourage which they will live. Of all the creatures on earth, you alone possess this gift. Only man can make the scenery change to match him.

By changing himself, he changes his territory. If a person understands this, he understands at the same time why he is master over everything else.

"You made him ruler over the works of Your hands; You put everything under his feet; all flocks and herds, and the beasts of the field, the birds of the air, and the fish of the sea."

Psalm 139

Man solves the riddles of the invisible germ, and travels at the speed of 200 hurricanes, swims to the bottom of the sea, and visits the universe. Yet, it is here we find this paradox. With this greatest gift of all, the majority of people neither know they have the gift, nor use it. The gift box is not even opened.

Sara Soda

Candy Cotton

I Hate Pink

Sara Soda: I think pink stinks!

Candy Cotton: I think green is mean!

Sara Soda: You just like to put on a show

Candy Cotton: You have hurt my feelings. Will you please go?

Sara Soda: Oh, I don't mean to be rude

Candy Cotton: No, you just insinuated I am invalid!

Sara Soda: Let me put it like this, "You're a snood!"

Candy Cotton: Well, I never! You are crude!

Sara Soda: Excuse me; are those freckles on your face?

Candy Cotton: To make fun of me is not your place!

Sara Soda: Well, you're quite a showcase

Candy Cotton: You need to go someplace!

Sara Soda: Do you have any friends?

Candy Cotton: A matter YOU can't comprehend!

Sara Soda: My friends do what I like

Candy Cotton: I would tell you to take a hike!

Sara Soda: If I make you mad will you turn another color?

Candy Cotton: You have already turned—green is for sour!

Sara Soda: I really do want a friend

Candy Cotton: Then can the insults end?

Sara Soda: I'm feeling really bad

Candy Cotton: Me too. This makes me sad.

Sara Soda: Can we forgive and...pray?

Candy Cotton: Let's do! Right away

Sara Soda: "Lord, I've been bad and I need you to forgive."

Candy Cotton: "Lord, I'm sorry...this is not the way to live."

Sara Soda: "You gave yourself as a sacrifice"

Candy Cotton: "To change the world and make us nice"

Sara Soda: "Thank you for answering prayer"

"Now love and kindness we will share."

(Together) Amen, Friend!   LOL

In Repair

Sara Soda: You have a big nose! It is longer than a hose

Candy Cotton: Your ears look like cauliflower, and your personality is sooo sour!

Sara Soda: Have you ever looked in the mirror?

Candy Cotton: Without a doubt, you're an insult bearer

Sara Soda: When I look at you, I have to blink twice

Candy Cotton: Did it ever occur to you to be nice?

Sara Soda: I'm just in awe at how husky you are.

Candy Cotton: Why you—you—you—sidecar!

Sara Soda: When I'm with you, you make me look good.

Candy Cotton: I've had it with you. You're really into selfhood.

Sara Soda: This friendship stinks. It smells like mildew.

Candy Cotton: And your insults I cannot outdo!

Sara Soda: What do you say we apologize? I know I'm right in my eyes

Candy Cotton: YOU I'm beginning to despise, but I'll give it a try

Sara Soda: Hey, are you coming down with pinkeye?

Candy Cotton: That's it; I don't want to be friends anymore

Sara Soda: Um, I'll apologize. Don't be sore

(Together) Lord help us to be someone to care. Someone to share. Together in prayer we'll forever declare our friendship is au pair. BFF!

Friendship Refined

Sara Soda: Something stinks. Is that your perfume?

Candy Cotton: No, you're smelling a skunk's tomb

Sara Soda: Yes, it does smell like something's dead

Candy Cotton: Oh, you're such an airhead

Sara Soda: I was thinking about you the other day-

Candy Cotton: Me too. It caused me great dismay

Sara Soda: Don't you know how to jostle?

Candy Cotton: Your humor is colossal.

Sara Soda: I was thinking how nice you look today

Candy Cotton: A return compliment is on delay

Sara Soda: Wouldn't it be nice to just talk to each other?

Candy Cotton: I'd much rather talk to another

Sara Soda: Okay. It's time to forgive and forget

Candy Cotton: Then I'd have so much regret

Sara Soda: Only the Lord can help us be friends

Candy Cotton: Maybe our attitude He can apprehend

Sara Soda: I know our friendship He'd improve

Candy Cotton: But you have a lotta trash He'd have to remove

Sara Soda: I know He can do miracles and wonders

Candy Cotton: And stop you from your blunders?

Sara Soda: That's the answer! We'll pray to Him

Candy Cotton: Maybe our friendship won't be so grim

Sara Soda: "This is the day the Lord has made"

Candy Cotton: We've come to you for a divine upgrade

Sara Soda: Thank you for hearing our prayer

Candy Cotton: We knew all along You'd be there."

IGBOK

IGBOK
(It's Going to Be Okay)

Peyton, the Painter

Painting the Palm Tree Marvel

I applaud the palm. It is a wonderment to me. Arabs and Egyptians could live ENTIRELY off the palm tree! Palms give fruit, dates, coconuts, and a sugary sap for beverage, which is used in sweet drinks and cooking oils. Its rich oil is used for soap, salad oils, margarine, cosmetics, and the wax from the leaves is used for shoe polish and formerly, phonograph records! Trunks are used for timber. Leaves are utilized for baskets, mats, brushes, and rattan furniture.

I have many, (to my dismay), silk palms in my studio. I have painted murals of palms. They are gorgeous and create a tropical ambience, for which I have a liking. Its shades of green are the color of progress. They grow straight and as much as 100 feet tall, as if they are reaching for the heavens. Nevertheless, they have roots that go deep in the soil. In hurricanes, the palm bends and gives itself to the storm. They are an endogen plant growing from within.

There is so much embodied in the painting of the palm. They are crowned with fruit and leaves. The older they are, the better the fruit is. And they sing. Yes, as the wind blows their one-of-a-kind leaves make a song for the passersby.

The palm says, "We make our own music." If you ask me what I came to do in this world, I, an artist, will answer you, I am here to live out loud.

We artists see things differently. If we did not, we would cease to be an artist. Inasmuch as palms are, by design, a source of the chief necessities of life with 360 different by-products, there are, incidentally, 1500 different kinds of palms! You may be getting a clue as to why I have amazement for this waving wonder.

Rarely do I paint with an exclusion of a palm branch some whither in the portrait, still life, animal picture, or commercial design.

And surmise Who has palm trees growing in His yard? There are palm trees in Heaven. John the Revelator penned,

"The glorified were described as clothed in white robes and with palms in their hands!"
Revelation 7:9.

Palm branches were spread in the streets as a "red carpet" to welcome Jesus into Jerusalem His last week on earth. This tree is a symbol of peace and victory, and it will be enjoyed throughout eternity.

An artist is not particularly keen on getting a thing done. He gets his pleasure from the process of doing it, playing with it, and fooling with it. The mere completion of it is an incident. The painting of the palm is relaxation, diversion, solace and pleasure. I have taken up with the palm for a very good reason:

"The righteous shall prosper like the palm tree."
Psalm 97:12

Not to Be Taken With a Grain of Salt

I have a riddle for you. It accompanies you at every meal. It is located on the table of the rich and the poor. It is put in place at every restaurant. There are no international boundaries and no language barriers with this article. It is vital to humanity, and I am intrigued with this condiment which we all savor.

What is it? I am delighted to paint one of the world's great salt mines in New Iberia, Louisiana, USA. It is a fascinating subject and as I paint the unimaginable landmark, I am awed. Let's talk salt!

At one time salt was a chief economic product of the ancient world. It was so scarce it was used as money. Caesar's army received part of their pay in common salt, known as "salarium." The word salary dates back to salt money. The modern expression "not worth his salt" literally means a person did not earn their wages.

Salt was used as a sign of honor, friendship, hospitality and purity. It was a religious custom of the Hebrews to rub newborn babies with salt to ensure good health. The European custom of throwing a pinch of salt over the left shoulder is a means of keeping the devil at a distance. Spilled salt signified a quarrel would soon take place. Salt means fellowship. The Arabs have an expression when visitors dine together, "There is salt between us, and we are friends."

In the Middle Ages a person's social rank was shown by whether he sat above or below the salt at the table. The higher ranks of society sat at a higher table, and the poor sitting at a lower level. It is not complimentary to be identified as "below the salt."

There is not a spread of color in this painting of the salt mines, and moreover, salt is flavorless. It is a mineral which has to be mixed with water in order to have taste. When mixed with saliva, it becomes a seasoning that brings excitement to bland foods.

Salt is a preservative. It is also an antiseptic with germ-killing properties for a mouthwash and gargle. Salt cures diseases in animals. There would be no ham, bacon, sausage gravy, or leather purses without the preserving properties of salt. It is also important to the development of the earliest highways of trade.

Roman soldiers built the Via Salaria (Salt Road) which led from Rome to the salt works of Ostia. Today, salt is used on highways to melt snow and ice for safer travel.

Much salt is obtained through evaporation by heat or the sun. There are more than 14,000 different uses for salt. All vital functions, including nerve impulses and heart action, depend on a salt and water balance. Perhaps we should ask forgiveness for taking salt for granted!

Even our vocabulary has been salted with this now common ingredient. We say; "below the salt", "salt a mine," "with a grain of salt" "salt away" and "salty". The Bible mentions salt more than 30 times and God hallmarks His followers as "the salt of the earth." Interesting.

I believe I am painting one of the wonders of the world when I paint a salt mine. Friend, can you please pass the salt?

The Signature Series

Paul Soldner, the famous potter, would deliberately destruct, batter, bang and slap his masterpieces. It is called "Anti-art." This professor precisely formed, slapped and bent his pieces, which was a reflection of the times. Picasso distorted his figures so they became unrecognizable. Not so with the potter who reveres the sanctity of my art. He has an idea in mind and toils at the potter's wheel to make a vessel of perfection. When it pleases him, he signs his name to each work of art!

I am intrigued with the origin of the potter's materials, that is, the clay itself. It is fine particles carried away from the parent rock and decomposed. Clay has fourteen elements the same as the human body. Perhaps that is the reason the clay challenges the potter, analogous to God and humanity. Clay can be very contrary. But the older the clay is, the better it is. In fact, Japanese bury their clay for future generations.

When I paint the magnificent work of a potter on my oil canvas, I am performing a work similar to a photographer. We both preserve the subject at hand. It is adding value to the potter's work and my brush compliments his craft. No two pieces of hand thrown clay are alike. It is my honor to paint art that cannot be duplicated, as in mass production.

This vase, with the potter's original technique, is unprecedented and marked. The artisan has a plan for the ideal vase, but the final details grow out of the actual process. The clay can be extremely uncooperative, to the point the potter must walk away from the process for a while. Sometimes he even pulls it from the wheel, reworks it, and throws it back on the wheel to begin again. "Man's task in life is to give birth to himself," (Erich Fromm 1947), and as an artist, I find greater pleasure in the act of painting than the finished picture. However, the potter's work is more laborious. He attains fulfillment with the completion of his unparalleled creation.

Walt Disney was known for his fabulous legendary masterworks and upon the perfection from the vivacity of his imagination, he ordered the team to "plus it." Their assignment was to surpass this marvelous undertaking. I like that philosophy. My brush should complement the object or individual. Perhaps the world's view should adopt such a credence as to add value to the people we make acquaintance with.

Not all clay will become a vessel of honor. Some clay will always be just dirt. Some will surround a burial site. Some clay will only be walked on. Clay cannot be used for planting because even weeds will not grow in it, but oh the clay that is brought from the miry pit, to be worked in a potter's hand, formed and shaped.

That chosen piece will be impressed with the designer's signature. My job, as a skilled painter, is to preserve the signature series which will grace the wall of architecture somewhere, someday.

The Disclaimer

The No Enemy Drink

If you feel all alone, despairing, uncared for, or abandoned to fate, then you suffer with the masses. Millions have no answer as to why they are victims of hopelessness. Are you experiencing discourtesy from strangers and even friends? Are there those who have been impossible to engage with, making drudgery in the workplace?

Closest relatives have become dreadful to be around. You want to dismiss friends from a calling list and dispose of them-at least temporarily. As far as you are concerned, you have fallen off the globe. Everything that is anything, is in extreme decline.

Good news! Listen to this. You can unmask a new example. For life's dilemmas there is an ultimate solution for heavy burdened individuals who lack courage to stand strong. What you need is the remarkable "No Enemy Drink!" It diminishes your enemies. It dispels the negatives in your life. You'll feel youthful, restored, and-yes-singing "Primrose Lane" where" life's a holiday!" The "No Enemy Drink" will relieve you from those unlovable people in your life.

Do not continue living in the gutter, head down, feet dragging, with a soured outlook on destiny. Imagine you without enemies and all those appalling people! Try the "No Enemy Drink." Do it now! Gulp it down! Your response to the despicable will be different. You will actually care and have empathy towards the former insidious.*

Disclaimer:

The "No Enemy Drink" is not for everyone, and there may be side effects. It does not change others. The transformation will only be in YOU! If you are asked for your coat, you will give your cloak also. If you are awakened in the night by a hungry homeless person, you will arise and give them what they need.

If you have qualms, you will forgive seventy times seven. If someone slaps you, you will turn the other cheek. You will lend to the poor and entertain strangers, because, possibly, they could be an angel unaware. You will pray for those who despitefully use you, and give a soft answer to an angry foe.

Your new radical social qualities can be overwhelming after consuming the "No Enemy Drink." If you experience breathing difficulties, dry mouth, tongue swelling, weakened limbs, faintness, or soup-bone syndrome, let your doctor know right away. Or better yet, you may need to contact your pastor or spiritual advisor.

*These statements have not been evaluated by the Food and Drug Administration. This product is not intended to diagnose, treat, cure, or prevent any disease.

Reclaimer:

Nevertheless, the ultimate authority Who is most reliable is humanity's Maker, Who issues a sure remedy. "Love your enemies" and practice The Golden Rule which is, "Do unto others as you would have them do unto you."

The Purple Passion Pill

So bored. Bored with life. Days of doldrums and monotony. Sick and tired of being sick and tired. Do you feel you are in a rut, weary, and indifferent about everything around you? Boredom: the desire for desires. A Dutch proverb says, "What the eye sees not, the heart craves." But it is said that it is easier to extinguish a first desire than to satisfy those that follow. Do not let life discourage you: everyone who got where he is had to begin where he was.

Every person's feelings have a front-door and a side-door by which they may be entered. The heart is inexperienced. We know too much and feel too little. This must change. Learn to manage your feelings by going through the side-door. It is accomplished through the Purple Passion Pill!

Want to rev up your engine and experience some acceleration? The Purple Passion Pill is just what you need! It will give you intensity of emotion and cravings to whet your appetite for excitement in your life. You haven't had that kind of eruption in a long time, have you? Steamed up and hot blooded for high powered stimulation, oh yeah!

To be passionless is for the aged and decrepit. Feel young again. Feel the fervency go through your veins. It is the pill that thrills! If you thought you could not be excitable, then the Purple Passion Pill is headlines for you. It is affecting thousands in all walks of life, all ages, and the retired are becoming refired! You can feel again! You can glow again! Get impassioned about life again! You cannot believe what you've been missing.

It is all in the C.I.A. of your mind. When you pick up speed in your thought life, you'll dispatch hi-speed emotion. The thrill of the thought and the ecstasy of the imagination come from the brain, the "home entertainment center."

This is known as "headquarters" for humans. Beware the central system affects all parts of the body and can be fatally dangerous if used in a non-discretionary way.

The Purple Passion Pill is the passage to feeling your exceptionalism as a human being.

Your new vigor will enrich your life with improvement, advancement, and endowment.
Everyone will notice and wonder what has enraptured you.

Do not delay because this is your day! Your fulfillment package is awaiting your decision to call. Order now. Supplies are limited. You must be at least 18 years old and bored to tears with life!

Disclaimer:

Some have reported a debilitating headache, vomiting, and insidious depression. Difficulty breathing, hives, tongue swelling and dry mouth and despondency of heart with descending self-esteem have been reported. Preoccupations with suicidal thoughts have been described. Do not take until the "Reclaimer" has been thoroughly read and understood.

Reclaimer:

It is most beneficial to a person seeking a thought-life makeover to be in compliance with the Bible's advice as noted in Philippians 4:8. "Whatsoever things are true, whatsoever things are honest, whatsoever things are just, whatsoever things are pure, whatsoever things are lovely, whatsoever things are of good report; if there be any virtue and if there be any praise, think on these things." Be advised all repairs, maintenance and sustenance are the Creator's specialties, since

He is the Maker.

The Forever Fruit
(A Re-count of the Beginning)

Agelessness. It is timelessness and nothing is final or completed or terminal. This place is the unending, undying "Infinite Forest and Gardens of Eden." It is the perpetual lap of luxury: An immeasurable gratification beyond one's imagination.

Can you be lonely? Oh no, never. Every classification, species, and genus are of linguistic cultism. Everything talks! The animals are euphonic with pomposity of speech. The grandiloquence of their experiences and stories could enrapture you for aeons. They are delightfully entertaining, and they are friendly.

You are close friends with the CEO of the Universe+ (plus, plus, plus...) You possess 100% brain power. You can be anything you want to be. You can do anything you want to do. You can go anyplace you want to go.

You are uninhibited in a shameless nudist colony, respectively. There is absolute unity with all inhabitants. Continual fulfillment, activism, excessive indulgence, and endless creature pleasures are the amenities of Eden.

The notorious Angel Choir perform concerts with the ambience of the beautiful forest and gardens. The trees clap their hands. The ocean keeps rhythm with the movement of the waves. The animal kingdom gives a unique sweetly flowing utterance and harmony unique to their kind. The sheep "baaa" in base tones.

The horses join in alto, "nay, nay." The hummingbird is melodious with the orchestration of birds in thousands of instrumental tones. The hyena fabulously adds soprano notes with other high-pitches. The parrots and like vocal birds get into the act with their plagiarist words. The alligator's tail and the elephant's trunk "swish-swish" as a drum beat. It is an all-inclusive symphony.

There is no end. What is there more in our world than anything else? Ends. And no time. But imagine Eve singing a song in the ultra-ultra affluent estate:

"One moment in time when all of my dreams are a heartbeat away...
One moment in time, and the answers are all up to me.
Give me one moment in time when I'm racing with destiny,
And in that one moment of time, I will feel eternity."

Written by Albert Hammond and John Bettis and sung by Whitney Houston

Then, impious I, offered one bite of the Forever Fruit. Just one bite, I say, and you will never die. You will have it all...Yes, the answer is up to you, and you are the master of your destiny.

One bite of the Forever Fruit and all this can be forever yours...

Disclaimer:

Physical death, separation from the CEO of the Universe+, work by the sweat of your brow, and till the ground with heavy labor. Pain in childbirth. Improvisation will be your lot. You will lose your home in Eden and you will be shamefully naked. You will now be afflicted with lust. The talking serpent will crawl on his belly and eat dirt forever. Didn't you almost have it all?

Reclaimer:

I will send my Son for the penalty for mankind's disobedience and to redeem and make a way for restoration to the Creator once again. His substitution on the cross for the punishment of all mankind will suffice in the transformation of the race. He must personally be accepted by each individual and the reconciliation is followed by obedience.

There is no other Name under heaven whereby man/woman can be saved. I have always loved you.

Megan, the Marathoner

Victory Mantras

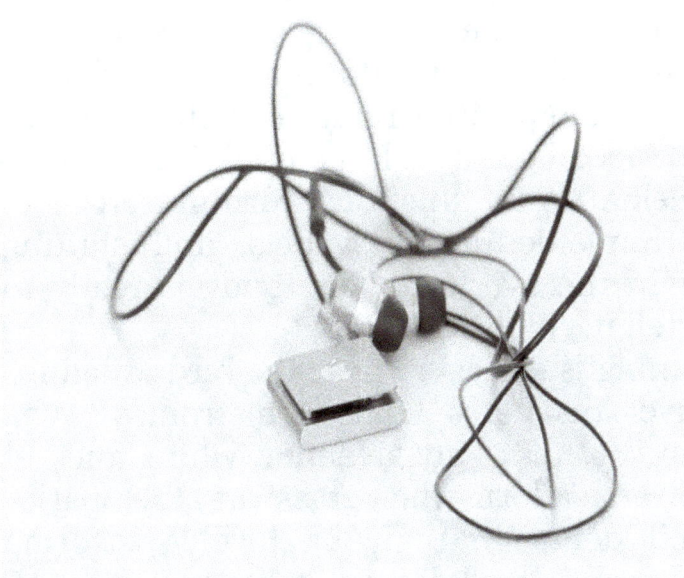

One for the money; two for the show; three to get ready, and go, Megan, go!

Mantras are various types of words and phrases that will distract the left side of the brain from its logical and, more than likely, negative thoughts. That is an energy thief. Mantras put you in a positive trance.

They are to be repeated over and over and will connect you to hidden resources that keep you going when you're tired.

Saucony's motto is a good one. "Find your strong!" Others are "Atta boy-go for it!" "You go girl!" "Be all you can be!" "Every day in every way I'm getting better and better."

The race is all about the ongoing commercials of the mind, promoting your ability to accomplish the feat. The brain is the control tower of the body. It gives continual orders, both subconsciously and consciously. This "headquarters" thrives on compliments and positive reinforcement. "I feel good. I feel fine. I feel like this-all the time!" The brain loves it and accelerates its functions, turning screws to all facilities, implementing movables, and shifting to high gear in the overhead. The body is ready to do what you tell it. WooHoo 26.2!

Running is ecstasy. I hear the birds singing. My MP-3 player resonates Louis Armstrong's "What A Wonderful World!" Tiny lavender, white, and yellow weed flowers adorn the grass at the park, an unexpected debut that give a lovely performance before they are mowed down. I smile as I think, "God, you love color, don't you?"

The sky is gorgeous. The sun is all-amazing. I gaze open-mouthed as it paints its first blush of the morning over the treetops. There is a slight wind in my face. This is heavenly! I can see. I can hear. I can taste. I can feel. I can move. I can smile! I am wondrously and marvelously created. My MP-3 player resounds, "Let the poor say I am rich. Let the weak say I am strong. Give thanks for all the Lord has done."

Oh, here comes my shadow! The song amuses my mind, "Me and my shadow...walking down the avenue."

I think to myself, "C'mon shadow, catch up with me. You can do it." Oh, she is a step ahead now. "Tryin' to outdo me, are you? " I have spunk. I have resolution, but my shadow has pertinacity! My alter ego moves to my right side then backs off, lagering behind. "C'mon, we're in this together!" But my silhouette disappears to the southeast.

There are only tree shadows where the sun is rising. My reflection appears again. "There's my partner!" Umbras come and go, but no matter, the pull of the finish line is movin' me right along.

There is a dead tree, the tallest in the park.

"Swoosh! Swoosh! It is six black buzzards with a six-foot wingspan swooping down on the running trail. A gaping audience of two remains at the top of the tree. This is scary. I pick up speed and watch them land and saunter around; relieved I'm not their target for breakfast. Now I feel comfortable and in control.

Entertaining a continual "Aha moment" in my mind, I think "I am happy. I feel good, I feel strong, I could run forever. This is fun. I'm on top of the world. I recall a little song from my childhood:

"I have something in my pocket-it belongs upon my face. I keep it in my pocket, in a most convenient place.

You'll never, never guess it, if you guess for a long, long while.

I will take it out and put it on. It is a great big runner's smile!"

My MP-3 player sounds the renowned Von Trapp's song, "Climb every mountain. Search high and low. Follow every byway, every path you know."

Friend, it is well with my soul.

The Athlete's Assessments

It is the unasked question, "How my doin'?" The athlete never asks that question, unless it is to have dialogue with the body. It is beneficial to assess yourself as you move in a race.

By evaluating your "motor parts" and "engine connections" you can pull yourself out of the motivational slump and energy leaks which usually happen at some point during long runs. The left brain bluffs and magnifies conditions to seem much worse than they really are. It tells me "Strength is almost gone" and says, "You may not finish," or "Better stop now before it gets worse." I talk back! It is as if my body is a duplex and two people are inside of me. One is destructive and the other constructive.

This is more than a race. The greatest enemy at any point in the marathon is not the stress, it is the internal doubt the left brain promotes. This negativism can be ignored by focusing on positive mental evaluations spotlighting success. A famous plastic surgeon and author, Maxwell Maltz, wrote a book on this idea titled Psycho Cybernetics. (that is, the machinery of the mind.)

The left side of the brain is logical with a million reasons to justify failure. The right side will not argue; but it will try to spur you on with its unlimited supply of creative and imaginative ways to steer you in the direction of your abilities.

The body is designed for forward motion. The forward motion creates positive momentum. A confident, positive manner helps engage the right brain. It bestows guttural confidence, which is intestinal fortitude, which is guts! You have an internal reservoir of fortitude. This source of strength comes directly from your spirit, which has the capacity to generate willful momentum.

Entertain the right brain and engage in assessments and self-talk. It is what you put in the forefront of your thoughts that counts. It goes like this:

This chariot is a magnificent running machine, and all moving parts are functioning with precision. Savor this moment. I feel good about what I'm doing. Enjoy the endorphins! I'm part of this monumental occasion. Benefits! Success! Achievement! Lookin' good! Proud! Strong! Better than ever! Negative messages cannot buffet me, because I am focusing on uncompromising control. I have veto power.

My body is in total synchrony. Arms swinging in harmony with footsteps. Chest feels good. Stomach receives snacks and pick-me-ups along the way. Water or sports drinks are offered every few miles. Smaller steps are relaxing my leg muscles. No cramps. Feet are a little numb, but I will change shoes for the last six miles. Ebenezer-"So far the Lord has helped me!" This body was created with superior excellence.

I am in charge of myself, a well-oiled running machine. This is my time to shine!

The Real Race

This is a big day for me. I'm registered for a marathon, 26.2 miles! I am decked out with running gear, my bib number, and the computer chip tracks my time. In moments the National Anthem will be played, the gun will fire, and thousands alongside me are off and running. This is exhilaration!

But the real race began the day I was born. The doctor gave me a spank on my bottom to welcome me into the hard-hat world. It must have been his way of saying, "You go, girl!" There are so many expectations for the newborn. There is eagerness for my weight gain to match other babies in the nursery.

Family anxiously coach for my first smile. I am expected to roll over, crawl, and take my first steps by a certain age. I must voice my first words as early as my cousins and Mother's friend's babies. Talk about pressure to perform! My beloved pacifier has to go by age two, because I am competing with others to "be big." At four years there may be pre-school, but definitely, kindergarten at five. Learning my ABC's and counting to 100 are mile markers along the way.

Moving right along, there is the first kiss at "sweet sixteen." (Or was it 'sweet sixteen and never been kissed?') Peer pressure. My graduation is foreseen and perhaps college awaits me. My counterparts and I pursue this road as we are eagerly watched. The audience applaud as my graduating class walk across the stage to accept the diploma. Now it is time to become...

I strive, mentor, worry, laugh and cry. I fall and pick myself up. There are tears, sweat and anxiety because of spectator's expectations. According to statistics, I have until 40 years old to increase my earnings to a higher level.

It is predicted I will marry and have a family actualized by mid-age, because soon I will no longer be childbearing. The insurance charts anticipate my life span. The assumptions in life's race are all predictable.

Life is a journey, a stroll for some, a sprint for others, and the long haul for most. The cheering and booing crowd is family, neighbors, educators, employers, and community. If I can keep my head up, my thoughts high, and my body under subjection, I think I can win this event. A sign is posted "Finish Line Ahead. Enter Through The Straight Gate."

The eternal reward is phenomenal: Commencement from mortality to immortality. I will probably sit down by the riverside, untie my running shoes, and say, "This was the best race I've ever had!"

It is Just Me, Pamela!

It is Just Me, Pamela!

Paper dolls were arranged all in a row on the bed awaiting their afternoon tea. They were part of my playtime reverie. I had a name for every one of them. I also told new friends about my five sisters. They were imaginary, but I had names for them, too. You see, I was an only child.

My world was one of make believe. Mother worked nights and slept days, Dad worked, and I lived in a world of quiescence. It was in those early years I developed an extraordinary imagination. I was a quietist, mostly.

We were a recreational family. My parents laced my first pair of roller skates when I was two and a half years old. They had met at a roller skating rink and skated for years after they married.

In my elementary years we went to the beach every day of the summer. Later when I was in junior high school, my parents bought a home on the lake. They bought a boat and we water skied frequently.

My parents were motivated people. Mother gave up twenty-one years seniority at Kellogg's and attended college to become a registered nurse. She was awarded "Nurse of the Year" in Michigan in the 1980's. Dad became the owner of a Mobil gas station. He painted cars on the side and I helped him mask the cars.

He instilled in me a fun desire to wash cars too, and I still like to wash my car! Dad took me to pick out flower bulbs so I could have my own garden in the back yard. They paid me one dollar a week to mow the yard and iron my dad's uniforms.

My mother taught me to thread her sewing machine and cut out a pattern. I made my first apron at age nine and took homemaking every year in school after that. I loved creating and designing. Funny, how the seeds that were sown in early years harvested in my adult life.

I had a repeated dream in childhood. I was ice-skating on a farm pond completely surrounded with overgrown bushes. It was very quiet and still. People were in the bushes watching me. Then suddenly all of them came out and were on the ice pond and there was noisiness, bustling, and dilemma.

It may have been the dream, but later I discovered something about myself. As I passed from childhood, I realized I was an ambivert. It is much like the ambidextrous person that functions well with either the right or left hand.

I can be introverted and quiet, but I can be extremely extroverted, craving recognition. I could sit in a woods for an hour, all alone, quiet with nature, or I could stand in front of a class campaigning for my election as vice president of the student council.

Then at age fourteen I had an encounter in a church at an altar. I met Jesus. He turned my life's hourglass upside down. Time and life had a new meaning. He took my black and white imagination and turned it to Technicolor.

He gave my anticipation a shot of heavenly steroids. My expectation was aroused to the force of faith. I do not live in a paper doll world anymore, but I am writing the lines to the story of my life. I do not really want to *be* somebody; I want to *meet* somebody. I want to cheer them, encourage them, and bring them a contagious smile.

And, perhaps, as the grains of sand slowly slip through that hourglass, *I will do just that!*

About the Author:

Pamela was married to "Captain Hook", (Von Saum) of "Pirate Adventures With Captain Hook", a television program for children airing over twenty years. She was "Mrs. Hook," the storyteller, costume designer, and script writer. The Captain went to heaven in 1993.

Remarried, Pamela and her husband Fred reside near Pensacola, Fl. They kayak, run, and bicycle together. Fred can construct anything, and she is a reservoir of ideas.

A good team! Together, they have five children and thirteen grandchildren.

www.ingramcontent.com/pod-product-compliance
Lightning Source LLC
Chambersburg PA
CBHW071305130626
46556CB00003B/1473